C000201619

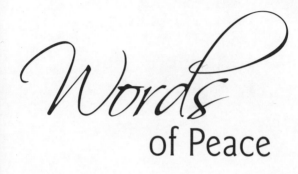

Words
of Peace

SELWYN HUGHES

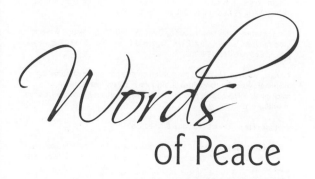

Words of Peace

POCKET DEVOTIONS

Needed – a new vision

FOR READING AND MEDITATION
ISAIAH 6:1–13

'In the year that King Uzziah died, I saw the Lord ...'
(v. I)

It is my conviction that perhaps more than at any other time in her history, the Christian Church needs *a fresh vision of God*. Almost without our realising it, a spiritual myopia has afflicted us; we are not seeing life clearly because we do not see God clearly. A right perspective on God gives us the right perspective on everything else – life, work, money, service, relationships, and so on. The tiniest of coins, when held close to the eye, can succeed in blotting out the sun. Our small problems can obscure God's glory in our lives. Isaiah came face to face with the living God and found that his whole life was transformed. I trust the same thing will happen to us as we pursue this theme together.

O God, give me in this new year, I pray, a fresh vision of You. I need it, and need it badly. Fill my whole horizon with the splendour of Your love, Your power and Your glory. Amen.

How sad!

FOR READING AND MEDITATION
ISAIAH 8:1–10

'... for God is with us.' (v.10)

When the king of Israel, Uzziah, died, a period of darkness suddenly descended on Israel, and in the midst of this spiritual despondency Isaiah was given a vision of the Lord high and lifted up and seated upon a throne. Was the fact that Isaiah's vision occurred soon after Uzziah's death a mere coincidence? I don't think so. In some way Uzziah's death triggered in Isaiah a spiritual crisis that made him more ready to lift his gaze from earth to heaven. How true to life this is. We look up only when something happens that knocks us flat on our backs. How sad that sometimes the earthly securities have to be removed before we can see the might and glory of Him who sits upon the throne.

Father, I am deeply sorry that I go through life with my gaze focused more on that which is around me than on that which is above me. Forgive me and help me develop a more heavenward gaze. Amen.

When props are knocked out

FOR READING AND MEDITATION
DEUTERONOMY 33:20–29

'The eternal God is your refuge and underneath are the everlasting arms.' (v.27)

I f Isaiah had been pinning his hopes for the spiritual survival of Israel on Uzziah rather than on God, then it is easy to see how disappointed and disillusioned he would have become on hearing that king Uzziah had died. I wonder: am I talking to someone right now who over the past year has had the props knocked from beneath their feet? The things you have depended on for so long are now no longer there. Then listen to me: God is not angry with you. He just wants you to rest your weight fully on Him. You may have to be willing to see your earthly securities laid in a coffin, so to speak, before you can see the glory of the One who sits upon the throne.

O Father, help me see that in all Your actions towards me, You have my highest interests at heart. You allow things to happen not to demean me, but to develop me. Give me a trusting heart. Amen.

Unchanging and unshakeable

FOR READING AND MEDITATION
HEBREWS 13:1–16

*'Jesus Christ is the same yesterday and today and for
ever.' (v.8)*

Every kingdom is shakeable except the kingdom of
God. The kingdom of communism is shakeable. It
has to be held together by force. Relax the force and, as
the world has witnessed, it goes to pieces. The kingdom
of finances is shakeable. The stock market goes up and
down with the international events of the day. The
kingdom of health is shakeable. The doctor says: 'I am
afraid you have an incurable sickness.' Shakeable! But in
a world of flux and change be assured of this – Christians
are people who belong to an unchanging Person and
who dwell in an unshakeable kingdom. God is allowing
kingdoms to be shaken so that they might discover the
unshakeable kingdom – the kingdom of God.

*Father, what a comfort it is to realise that I belong to an
unchanging Person and an unshakeable kingdom. Passing
events cannot shake me. I am eternally grateful. Amen.*

'I saw the Lord'

FOR READING AND MEDITATION
EXODUS 24:1–18

'… and saw the God of Israel.' (v.10)

A ll systems that leave out Jesus Christ are doomed to failure, for they are not in harmony with the universe. Probably the greatest form of evangelism that is going on at the moment is the shaking of the nations. What is shakeable is being shaken so that the unshakeable might appear. God is preparing the world for the revelation of His kingdom in a way that many cannot see or understand. But what about your own personal life? Is that being shaken? Take heart – all this could be the prelude to a new vision of God. God has often to empty the throne of our hearts before He fills it with Himself. You may yet say: 'In the year that all my hopes and expectations came crashing down … *I saw the Lord.'*

O Father, how I long that this year will become for me a year of vision and venture. Show me Your glory, I pray, in a way that I have never known before. Amen.

Whose universe is this?

FOR READING AND MEDITATION
HEBREWS 1:1–14

'But about the Son he says, "Your throne, O God, will last for ever and ever …"' (v.8)

We move on now to consider the fact that when Isaiah received his vision of God he saw the Almighty 'seated on a throne' (Isa. 6:1). Why a throne? *To reassure him whose universe it was.* A king reigns from a throne. It is the symbol of might, power and authority. It was as if God was saying to Isaiah, 'There may be no one on the throne of Israel at this moment, but My throne is never unoccupied and never unattended.' We too need at this critical hour in human history to be sustained by the vision of the Almighty 'seated upon the throne'. The throne of God is unassailable. Take the text that is at the top of this page and let it ring again in your heart: 'Your throne, O God, will last for ever and ever.'

My Father and my God, just as You have sustained others with a vision of Your throne – sustain me too, I pray. Your throne is unassailable and unimpeachable. Thank You, Father. Amen.

Our God reigns!

FOR READING AND MEDITATION
PSALM 9:1–20

'… you have sat on your throne, judging righteously.'
(v.4)

The kingdoms of Europe have been shaken in order that from the dust the unshakeable kingdom might appear. Christians should remember that it is from the throne of heaven, not the thones of earth, that the final decisions are made regarding the world's affairs. There are times when it looks as if the authority of heaven's throne has little to do with what transpires on planet Earth. Murder, pillage, lust, greed, rape, selfishness, pride and jealousy are spread wide across it, and the battle between good and evil seems as sharp as ever. But don't be taken in by what you see with your eyes or read in your newspapers. Appearances may be unconvincing, but our trust is in the God who reigns.

Father, I bow in Your presence and acknowledge You as the ruler of the universe and the captor of my heart. Amen.

Why doesn't God do something?

FOR READING AND MEDITATION
PSALM 10:1–18

'Why, O Lord, do you stand far off? Why do you hide yourself in times of trouble?' (v.1)

Many people, most of whom live their normal lives in neglect of God, complain in times of distress or national emergency that God never seems to do anything. Even the psalmist struggled with this question. There is only one answer to be given to this question – *God does not work our way.* This may not satisfy some, but it is an answer nevertheless. His might finds fitting expression not in the power to wound, but in the power to woo. His power is not coercion but constraint. Never does He violate the personalities He has made. It would be easy for Him to intervene, but another purpose is at work – the purpose of constraining love. Hard though it may be, we must have patience with the patience of God.

Father, help me see and understand this important truth that in running the world You do not work our way. I am big enough to ask questions but not big enough to understand the answers. Amen.

Unassailable – but accessible

FOR READING AND MEDITATION
HEBREWS 4:1–16

*'Let us then approach the throne of grace with confidence
…' (v.16)*

Though God reigns from a majestic throne, He is accessible to us at all times of day and night. The lines of communication that lead from us to Him are never blocked and never 'down'. When a man or woman, boy or girl says, 'God be merciful to me a sinner', the message goes straight through to the throne and they receive this personal reply: 'You are forgiven, redeemed and set free from your sin.' The throne of God, you see, is not only a throne of righteousness but a throne of *grace*! Righteousness says, 'Stay back until you are good enough to approach.' Grace says, 'I will put on you the robes of righteousness that are provided for you by Christ – now you are good enough.' Too good to be true? Too good not to be true!

Father, I draw near again today to Your throne of grace, and with the redeemed all around the world sing: 'How marvellous, how wonderful is my Saviour's love to me.' Amen.

The sceptre of righteousness

FOR READING AND MEDITATION
ESTHER 5:1–14

'So Esther approached and touched the tip of the sceptre.'
(v.2)

What a beautiful picture this is of the way we sinners are accepted into the presence of the King of kings. We are told in Hebrews 1:8 that God too has a sceptre – a sceptre of righteousness – which soiled sinners would never be able to touch. However, the good news of the gospel is this: we can approach the throne of a holy God with the assurance that through the sacrifice on the cross, God has given us His righteousness. God holds out to us His sceptre of righteousness – the finished work of Christ – and as we move forward and touch it, in other words acknowledge our acceptance of it, we are welcomed into His presence as if we had never sinned. And it's all because of Jesus. Blessed be His name for ever!

O Father, how can I sufficiently thank You for extending to me Your offer of salvation in Christ? What amazing mercy! What wondrous grace! Help me witness to it both by my lips and by my life. Amen.

'His Majesty!'

FOR READING AND MEDITATION
PSALM 95:1–11

'For the LORD is the great God, the great King above all gods.' (v.3)

What is the word that immediately comes to mind when you think of a throne? Is it not the word 'majesty'? Our word 'majesty' comes from the Latin and means 'greatness'. 'Majesty' is a word that is often used of God. Why was it necessary and important for Isaiah to see God 'seated on a throne'? Because his instincts of trust and worship would be stimulated by a vision of God's greatness and majesty. And so it will be with us. One of the reasons why our faith is so flabby and feeble is because our thoughts of God are not great enough. Learn to associate God with majesty. I promise you, filling your mind with thoughts of 'His Majesty' will set your devotional life on fire!

O Father, as I turn my gaze upward to focus on Your greatness and Your glory, set my soul on fire. I look at You and my heart cries out in godly reverence and fear: 'Your Majesty'. Amen.

Difficulties – not almighty

FOR READING AND MEDITATION
ISAIAH 28:16–29

'... the Lord, the Lord Almighty, has told me ...' (v.22)

I t is so easy for us to allow the problems of life to loom large and great in our thinking, and soon we lose the right perspective on things. Things like economic recession, international tension and political change can become issues that almost blot out God. Maybe someone you trusted has hurt you, walked out on you and deserted you, and that problem has become so large that it reaches almost cosmic proportions. Well, I want to tell you today that, big though it may be, it is not bigger than God. Don't lose your perspective. The Lord is on His throne, high and exalted. See how big God really is and set your problems over against that vision. Your difficulties are not almighty. *The Lord alone is almighty.*

O God, fill my vision with Yourself, for I see that when I do not view You as almighty I can so easily view my problems in that way. Keep my gaze and my focus fully on You. Amen.

Seeing God as God

FOR READING AND MEDITATION
ISAIAH 40:1–20

'Whom did the LORD consult to enlighten him ... Who was it that taught him knowledge ...?' (v.14)

Here Isaiah asks two questions designed to correct wrong thoughts about God. We think of God as too much like ourselves. Put the mistake right, says Isaiah. Learn to acknowledge the full majesty and greatness of God. Isn't it sad that because we ourselves are limited and weak, we imagine that, at some points, God is too, and find it hard to believe that He is not. Isaiah does here what a doctor would do when entering the room of a sick patient who has closeted himself behind shuttered windows. He opens the windows, lets in the fresh air and light and says, 'No wonder you are sick, you are not linking yourself enough to the resources that bring healing.' Spiritual health comes from seeing God as He is.

My Father and my God, if I am mistakenly making You in my image, forgive me. Help me see You as You really are – ruling and reigning with all might, all power and all authority. In Jesus' name. Amen.

Strength like the eagle's

FOR READING AND MEDITATION
ISAIAH 40:21–31

'They will soar on wings like eagles ...' (v.31)

Isaiah's third question is: 'Why do you say, O Jacob, and complain, O Israel, "My way is hidden from the Lord; my cause is disregarded by my God?"' The previous questions were designed to correct the wrong thoughts the Israelites had about God; this one is designed to correct the wrong thoughts they had about themselves. They were allowing themselves to think that God had abandoned them. Fourthly he asks if they are aware that God never gets tired and has unimaginable wisdom. This question is designed to rebuke them for their slowness to believe in God's greatness and majesty. He talks to them in a way that is calculated to shame them out of their unbelief. As we quietly contemplate God's majesty, our strength is renewed.

Father, as I wait before You now, write these truths upon my heart so that I shall be gripped by these important convictions. I don't just want to hold them as ideas; I want them to hold me. Amen.

'He is exalted ...'

FOR READING AND MEDITATION
PSALM 92:1–15

'But you, O Lord, are exalted for ever.' (v.8)

We move on now to focus on a further phrase that Isaiah uses when describing his vision of God: 'I saw the Lord ... *high and exalted*' (Isa. 6:1, my italics). The words 'seated on a throne' introduce us to the majesty of God; the words 'high and exalted' introduce us to the transcendence and loftiness of God. These words take us beyond the fact that God is seated on a throne and show us that His throne is situated far above the boundaries of space and time. Oh how desperately we need a new vision of the transcendence of God in the Church of today. To truly worship God we need to see that we are worshipping Someone who is not only above us, but transcends far above us. He is the Creator – we are merely creatures.

Father, help me see that while You are nearer to me than the breath I breathe, You are also a God who is high and exalted. In Jesus' name I pray. Amen.

Immanent – yet transcendent

FOR READING AND MEDITATION
ISAIAH 57:11–21

*'I live in a high and holy place ... with him who is
contrite and lowly in spirit ...' (v.15)*

The idea behind transcendence is that of
distinctiveness, separateness – that God is uniquely
other than everything in creation. Over against that
thought we must hold the truth of God's immanence,
and by that we mean that He dwells in the lives of those
who have repented of their sin – a truth our text for
today brings out so clearly. The fact that God indwells
us must not be allowed to cloud the truth that He is
above us, infinitely exalted above all creation. To think
of God as transcendent inspires adoration and worship.
Without this idea in our minds, worship is a mere ritual
and a formality. With it, worship is vibrant and full of
meaning.

*O God, forgive me if, in my desire to have You close to me,
I have lost sight of Your majesty, Your greatness and Your
transcendence. Help me to see You as high and exalted.
Amen.*

'The proper study of mankind ...'

FOR READING AND MEDITATION
JOHN 17:1–19

'Now this is eternal life: that they may know you, the only true God ...' (v.3)

I think that, notwithstanding all the good things happening in the Church of today, there is not enough teaching and emphasis on the nature and character of God. The contemporary Church, generally speaking, focuses more on issues such as 'good self-image' or 'effective prayer' than it does on how to know God. Not that these other issues are unimportant but, as Jim Packer says in his book *Knowing God*: 'Knowing God is crucially important for the living of our lives. The world becomes a strange, mad, painful place, and life in it a disappointing and unpleasant business, for those who do not know about God.'

Father, I see that knowing You better involves increased time – time to talk to You and time for the study of You. Guide me in my knowledge of You. In Jesus' name I pray. Amen.

Our prayers reveal us

FOR READING AND MEDITATION
DANIEL 9:1–19

'O Lord, the great and awesome God ...' (v.4)

We must be careful not to think of God as highest in an ascending order of beings, starting with a single cell and going on up from, say, a fish to a bird, to a man, to an angel, to an archangel, and then God. This would be to see God merely as eminent, perhaps even pre-eminent, but He is so much greater than that. He is transcendent. The amoeba and the archangel, though far removed from one another in the scale of created things, are, nevertheless, one in that they are both created. If you want to know how a person thinks about God, listen to him or her pray! It's interesting to note that those who know God intimately invariably begin by acknowledging His greatness and transcendence.

O God, slowly the light is dawning – when You are not in Your place then everything else is not in place. You can get along without me, but I can't get along without You. Amen.

God help grammar!

FOR READING AND MEDITATION
PSALM 46:1–11

'Be still, and know that I am God ...' (v.10)

I would like to repeat an ungrammatical question posed by a famous preacher: Have *you* a God you can be still with? He ended a sentence with a *preposition*, but it is the *proposition* that is important. In other words, is your life such a ceaseless round of activity that when you come to focus your mind on God you cannot give yourself to the task for very long, so you blurt out a few prayers and then you are gone? You won't get to know God – really know God – that way. You see, what the text before us today is saying is this: you cannot get to know God until you are willing to stay still before Him. Knowing God means attending to Him, contemplating Him, worshipping Him, meditating upon Him and studying Him.

Loving heavenly Father, help me face up to and not rush past the question: 'Have I a God with whom I can be still?' Slow me down, dear Father, so that I face this issue. In Jesus' name. Amen.

Knowing God as He is

FOR READING AND MEDITATION
JOHN 4:1–26

'God is spirit, and his worshippers must worship in spirit and in truth.' (v.24)

It is impossible to follow Christian principles in our lives and perform our Christian duties properly when our attitudes towards God or our view of Him is wrong. If we are to see spiritual power and energy flowing through our lives then we must begin to think of God *as He is*, not as we would like Him to be. A true understanding of God is as important to our worship of God, our work for God and our witness to God as a foundation is to a building. If the foundation is not right then the building will be lopsided or, worse, will topple over. Worship of God must always come before effective work for God. What kind of building will the Church of the next generation inherit from us? A strong one or an unsteady one?

O God, I long with all my heart to worship you 'in spirit and in truth'. And whatever the roadblocks on that journey, help me remove them and overcome them. Amen.

Christian idolaters

FOR READING AND MEDITATION
PSALM 48:1–14

'Within your temple, O God, we meditate on your unfailing love.' (v.9)

The idolatrous heart assumes that God is other than He is, and substitutes for the true God one made after its own imagining. But a god created out of our imagination is not the true God. God has given us a clear picture of Himself in the Scriptures, but when we continue to hold wrong ideas of Him, preferring to see Him the way we think He should be rather than the way He is, we libel His character and demean Him. If we try to worship the god of our own imagining we then commit idolatry, for we are not worshipping the true God at all, we are worshipping our idea of Him drawn from the darkness of our minds. If we have a mental image of God that is different from God we become Christian idolaters.

O Father, help me draw my concept of You from Your Word and from Your revelation in Christ, not from the mists of my own misconceptions. In Jesus' name. Amen.

Our biggest single problem

FOR READING AND MEDITATION
JOHN 14:1–14

'Anyone who has seen me has seen the Father.' (v.9)

The biggest single problem I have come across in the lives of fellow Christians is disappointment with God because of something He did not do, or something He did not provide. The cause – a wrong understanding of God and His ways. I have heard people say: 'I asked God to give me patience and instead He allowed the pressures to increase.' 'I asked God to take away my anger towards my wife and children, but He failed to answer my prayer.' The sooner we learn to accept God as He is, not as we would like Him to be, the sooner we will move from the path of confusion to confidence. I tell you, this is a matter of supreme importance.

O Father, help me know You better so that my expectations are based on truth, not on wishful thinking. In Jesus' name I pray. Amen.

The bottom line

FOR READING AND MEDITATION
HABAKKUK 1:1–17

'How long, O LORD, must I call for help, but you do not listen …?' (v.2)

The reason so many Christians become disappointed with God is because they do not have what can best be described as a 'bottom line' – a line we draw under God that best explains Him to us. The 'bottom line', as it relates to God, is not deliverance or healing or protection or any similar thing. He demonstrates and exercises His ability to do these things from time to time, but they are not to be seen as inevitable. Sometimes He heals and sometimes He doesn't. Sometimes He delivers and sometimes He doesn't. Sometimes He protects us from afflictions and accidents, and at other times He allows them to happen. Even Habakkuk confessed that he could not understand why God did not come through for His people.

Father, help me move, as Habakkuk did, from confusion to confidence, and give me the understanding and convictions I need to trust You even when I cannot trace You. Amen.

Steady as you go!

FOR READING AND MEDITATION
HABAKKUK 3:1–19

'The Sovereign LORD is my strength; he makes my feet like the feet of a deer ...' (v.19)

Following on from our meditations yesterday, I suggest the 'bottom line' in God is His justice. By that I mean the truth that whatever God does, He does because it is right. Not that it is right because God does it, but that God does it because it is right. There is a world of difference between those two things. Habakkuk comes to see that whatever God does is just, and it is his new-found confidence in the justice of God that holds him steady as he contemplates the judgment that God is about to bring on His people. I tell you, with all the conviction of my heart, that unless we are gripped by the belief that God acts justly in everything – *everything* – then we will not have the sure-footedness we need to negotiate the rocky slopes that are up ahead.

Father, I see that if I am to move upwards in my Christian life with the sure-footedness of a deer, then I can only do so as I am gripped by the conviction that everything You do is right. Amen.

'My comfort is my justice'

FOR READING AND MEDITATION
EZEKIEL 14:12–23

*'They will come to you, and when you see their conduct
and their actions, you will be consoled ...' (v.22)*

God tells Ezekiel that He is going to bring judgment
upon Jerusalem, but that He would provide
comfort during that destruction and Ezekiel would be
consoled. The 'bottom line' is not comfort but justice,
demonstrated in this case by God's punishment of
evildoers. By justice I mean God doing what is right
in each and every situation. God has a just cause for
everything He does. Sometimes in life things do not go
the way we expect them to go. Spiritual maturity is seen
in us when we say with Abraham, when he was pleading
with God for the deliverance of Sodom: 'Shall not the
Judge of all the earth do right?' (Gen. 18:25, AV). If your
'bottom line' is drawn at *your* idea of justice, not God's,
His actions are anathema to you.

*Father, help me resolve this tension between my idea
of justice and Yours, otherwise I shall continue to
misunderstand – even rebel. Teach me to accept that Your
way is right – always. Amen.*

'See His glory come down'

FOR READING AND MEDITATION
ISAIAH 48:1–11

'I will not yield my glory to another.' (v.11)

We tend to demand from God not real justice but justice on our own terms – our terms being deliverance, healing or divine protection. When will we ever get away from the idea that our wellbeing is the foundation and cause for divine justice? We must never put our wellbeing or glory before God's. There is a much higher value in this universe than our glory – it is God's glory. If we are going to develop any degree of spiritual maturity in our lives, then we are going to have to put a higher value on God's glory than our own wellbeing. If we don't, then we will never come to know the depth of trust that Job exhibited when he said: 'Though he slay me, yet will I hope in him' (Job 13:15).

Father, help me understand that in putting Your glory before my wellbeing I do not demean myself but develop myself. For in glorifying You I too am glorified. Help me grasp this. Amen.

Where is our trust?

FOR READING AND MEDITATION
PSALM 62:1–12

'Trust in him at all times ...' (v.8)

The biggest problem we carry in our souls is not the pain that others have inflicted upon us, but the pain we have inflicted (and continue to inflict) upon God. Let me spell out as clearly as I can exactly what I mean. Many Christians are far more interested in focusing on how they can get God to comfort them when they have been hurt than considering how much they have hurt Him. Not that it is wrong to seek His comfort – Scripture encourages us to do this – but it is only one side of the picture. If someone upsets us and we decide to upset them in return, that is a violation of a divine principle which is sin and hurts God. Instead we should commit ourselves to God and seek His glory in every situation.

O God, forgive me that I am more concerned about how others have acted towards me than the way I act towards You. I see that a failure to trust You is a failure in love. Forgive me and help me. Amen.

Close – but not close enough

FOR READING AND MEDITATION
PSALM 86:1–17

'Teach me your way, O LORD … give me an undivided heart …' (v.11)

Instead of trying to get back at others, we may withdraw from them and decide never again to give them an opportunity to hurt us. We relate to them at a superficial level – close enough to be considered friendly or sociable, but not close enough to get hurt. But God says, 'If your enemy is hungry, feed him; if he is thirsty, give him something to drink … Do not be overcome by evil, but overcome evil with good' (Rom. 12:20–21). What this text is saying, you see, is this – *be concerned about the person who has hurt you and put that concern into action; get close to them again and risk being hurt again.* How sad that we are more keen to preserve our own wellbeing than to seek God's glory by obeying His Word.

O God, we do not see ourselves, for we look at the sins that others commit against us with open eyes and then turn a blind eye upon the sins we commit against You. Help us to be honest. Amen.

'Come on, Lord, act justly'

FOR READING AND MEDITATION
DEUTERONOMY 32:1–12

'… all his ways are just. A faithful God … upright and just is he.' (v.4)

'To dwell only on the fact that we have been victimised,' says Larry Crabb, 'is to develop a demanding spirit.' We tend then to say to God: 'Come on, Lord, start acting justly and defend me against my adversaries. Command fire to fall down upon their heads!' Once we give up our demanding attitude, however, we are at the mercy of other people and have to go through life trusting God to deal with them on His terms. Can we handle that kind of vulnerability? I am not suggesting that people who experience serious abuse ought not to report it to the authorities. What I have in mind is that we focus more on how much we have hurt God, and then on what others have done to us. As we do this, what others have done seems of much less significance than what we have done to God.

Gracious Father, forgive us for the wrongs we inflict upon ourselves by trying to live in ways other than Your way. Help us to take Your way unreservedly. Amen.

Hearing *and* seeing!

FOR READING AND MEDITATION
JOB 42:1–17

'My ears had heard of you but now my eyes have seen you.' (v.5)

Perhaps the greatest example of a failure to understand God's justice is Job. Job came to believe that the whole of life was unfair. However, he eventually began to see that any movement against God's justice is a heinous sin. Job's previous problem of being mistreated and misjudged is forgotten in the light of the greater problem that he had misjudged the Almighty. As Job prayed for the friends who hadn't been much help to him and as he turned the focus from himself to others, something wonderful took place within him – his rebellion dissolved and he was delivered from all his problems. Job came to see God *as He is*, not just as he wanted Him to be.

O Father, to hear of You by ear is indeed wonderful, but to 'see' You is bliss beyond compare. Bring me to the same place You brought your servant Job – no matter what lies in between. Amen.

Too far to turn back

FOR READING AND MEDITATION
PSALM 73:1-28

'Whom have I in heaven but you? And being with you, I desire nothing on earth.' (v.25)

One of the things that prevents us from seeing God as He really is is our preoccupation with how others behave towards us, rather than the way we have behaved towards God. Those who really know God show little concern about what others have done to them; they are too busy focusing on how they can arrive at a better knowledge of Him. They brood not on what they have missed, but on what they have gained; not what might have been, but how far they have come. Every one of us must get hold of the fact that a little knowledge *of* God is worth more than a great deal of knowledge *about* Him. Thus we must pursue the vision that the young Isaiah received in the temple still further. We have come too far to turn back now.

Father, at last the doors of my life are beginning to turn outward instead of inward. I am beginning to focus more on You than on myself. Lead me on, my Father. I shall follow. Amen.

The exclusiveness of God

FOR READING AND MEDITATION
1 PETER 2:1–12

'… and the one who trusts in him will never be put to shame.' (v.6)

We come now to the phrase: 'And the train of his robe filled the temple' (Isa. 6:1). The thought being conveyed here is the exclusiveness of God. There was no room for anyone else in this high exalted place. God was all in all. So many of us have a faith in God that goes something like this: God *and* a good job; God *and* good health; God *and* a loving family; God *and* a big bank balance. All of these things are fine as desires, but when they become demands, we are tipping our hand as to where our real trust lies. Let me ask you this question: Is God sufficient in your life? Is God enough or are there competing desires for the first place of affection in your heart?

O Father, forgive me that so often I lean on my own self-sufficiency or the sufficiency of others more than on You. With all my heart I affirm it – You are my sufficiency. Amen.

God 'and' …

FOR READING AND MEDITATION
COLOSSIANS 2:1–15

'… and you have been given fullness in Christ …' (v.10)

When the Lord divided Canaan among the tribes of Israel, Levi received no share of the land. God said to him: 'I am your inheritance' (Num. 18:20). Those words made Levi richer than all his brethren, and this principle holds good for every child of God. The man or woman who knows God has the world's greatest treasure. He or she may not have many earthly treasures, but it will not make much difference, for in having Him they have everything that matters. Do we look at the Lord who promises to be our portion and find that He is sufficient? Or are we still caught up with the idea that we need God and something else? If we do then we do not really know God. We simply know about Him.

O Father, help me remember that I belong to You, the all-creative, all-sufficient God. Make this truth come alive for me, not just in my head but in my heart too. In Jesus' name I pray. Amen.

No other gods

FOR READING AND MEDITATION
EXODUS 20:1–21

'You shall have no other gods before me.' (v.3)

Why did God say: 'I am the Lord your God. You shall have no other gods before me'? And why does He still challenge us with that word when we want to make our gods of wood or stone? Of silver and of gold? Of fame and fortune? The reason is that there are no other gods. We are fooling ourselves. We can give ourselves to them but they can't give themselves to us. This is how it is with the gods of this world. We think they can deliver, but they let us down every time. So I ask you again: do you look at the Lord who promises to be your inheritance, your portion, and see Him as sufficient? Or do you sometimes lose perspective and look at other gods? Remember – *there are no other gods.*

O God, forgive me for the times I turn from You to lesser gods. You alone are God, and in all my life, individual and social, I bow my knee to You. In Jesus' name. Amen.

God – the Enough!

FOR READING AND MEDITATION
GENESIS 17:1–22

'… I am God Almighty (El Shaddai) …' (v.1)

The Hebrew term for God, 'El Shaddai', means 'God – the Enough!' That phrase – 'the Enough' – brings home to the heart the truth that there is no situation in which we will ever find ourselves where God will not be enough. There are many things in the world of which we think we do not have enough – money, power, status, education, and so on. And it is generally assumed that if only it were possible to have a sufficiency of 'things', satisfaction would immediately result. But that is not so. The real trouble is not that people do not have enough 'things', but that the 'things' in themselves are not enough. Only God is sufficient for us; only He can truly satisfy our souls. He, and only He, is enough.

O Father, save me from thinking that anything can ever be a substitute for You. Just as Your glory filled all the temple in Isaiah's day, so let Your glory fill me – exclusively. Amen.

An encounter with the holy

FOR READING AND MEDITATION
ISAIAH 33:10–24

'Who of us can dwell with the consuming fire?' (v.14)

The Hebrew word for 'seraph' in Isaiah 6:2 means 'burning ones' or 'noble ones', those whose specific ministry is to stand before the throne of God and offer up continuous worship. Ancient Christian writers often referred to a close encounter with God as like entering a danger zone. What did they mean? One author interprets it like this: 'If we are sinful and God is holy, if God is a fire and we are straw, how can it be safe for us to enter His presence? The fact is, it is not safe. It is exceedingly dangerous.' The closer we get to God the more we run the risk of all that is unlike Him being consumed and destroyed. But when you think of it – isn't that the very reason why we ought to yearn to draw close to Him?

O Father, I see that this is something I cannot have too much of – an encounter with the holy. Draw me, for I want to get as close as I can to Your holy fire. In Jesus' name. Amen.

Lost and found

FOR READING AND MEDITATION
HEBREWS 12:14–29

*'… let us be thankful, and so worship God acceptably
with reverence and awe …' (v.28)*

Why did the seraphs cover their faces? Clearly
they dared not look upon this One whom they
were worshipping and serving. The implication here is
that what we do for God must be done with reverence.
One of the tragedies of modern-day Christianity is that
quietly and almost unnoticed we are losing the spirit of
reverence. Holy things are becoming treated as common
and are losing their sacredness. It is not happening
everywhere, of course, but there is no doubt in my
mind that the cynicism of the age through which we are
passing is making an impact on the Christian Church.
We dare not lose our reverence for holy things. Too
much is at stake.

*O God, help me develop respect and reverence for holy
things without becoming over-spiritual and mystical. Keep
me balanced. In Jesus' name. Amen.*

'God's beautiful people'

FOR READING AND MEDITATION
ISAIAH 52:1–15

'How beautiful … are the feet of those who bring good news …' (v.7)

The seraphs also covered their feet. The implication here is that what is done for God must be done with humility. Someone has pointed out that the only thing that is said to be 'beautiful' about the followers of the Lord in Scripture is not their faces or their figures, but their feet! That ought to keep us humble – if nothing else does. God has His 'beautiful' people – those who carry the good news of the gospel wherever they go. The seraphs did not focus attention on themselves but on the Lord whom they were serving. We ought never to forget that as far as our service for Christ is concerned, our task is not to draw attention to ourselves but to Him. And it is not possible to do both at the same time.

Father, in all my service for You may I be hidden behind the cross, so that the voice people hear will not be mine alone, but the still small voice of the Holy Spirit speaking to them. Amen.

Pursuing with passion

FOR READING AND MEDITATION
PSALM 16:1–11

'The sorrows of those will increase who run after other gods.' (v.4)

The seraphs flew with two of their wings. The implication here is that our service and our worship for God must be done with urgency. Few Christians seem to chase after God; they choose rather to saunter after Him. Christian service, generally speaking, is characterised more by lethargy than urgency, more by indolence than inspiration and more by fitfulness than fervency. Contrast this with the people who serve the gods of sex, pleasure, fame, money and so on. There is hardly a demand their gods make upon them that seems to be too much. They are willing to give up sleep, stay out until the early hours and spend any amount they have to in order to satisfy their gods. We must serve God with urgency and passion.

O God, how can I ever thank You enough for pursuing me with urgency and passion? Grant that my passion might match Your passion. Amen.

Our primary task

FOR READING AND MEDITATION
PSALM 29:1–11

'Ascribe to the LORD the glory due to his name; worship the LORD in the splendour of his holiness.' (v.2)

The seraphs in Isaiah's vision were worshipping God. 'Holy, holy, holy is the Lord Almighty; the whole earth is full of his glory' (Isa. 6:3). What is worship? The essential meaning of the word in both Old and New Testaments is that of reverential service – a truth we saw illustrated by the winged seraphs before the eternal throne. Our present-day English word 'worship' has evolved from the Anglo-Saxon *weorthscipe*, which means 'to give worth' to someone or something. Worship can best be understood by thinking of the word in this way: worth-ship. The worship of God then is attributing worth to Him, reflecting on Him, thinking about Him – *and only Him.*

Father, I ask myself in Your presence: how much of my life is spent in worship? Help me draw near to You, not just to ask for things, but just to worship You. In Jesus' name I pray. Amen.

'A constant pageant of worship'

FOR READING AND MEDITATION
REVELATION 7:1–17

'… and serve him day and night in his temple …' (v.15)

We must be careful not to fall into the trap of differentiating between worship and service, and thinking to ourselves that when we kneel in private we are at worship and when active in the church, such as teaching, preaching or being of some practical help, we are then engaged in service. All service is worship, and all worship is service. In the book of Revelation, heaven is seen as a place that is filled with worship but it is also a place where the saints 'serve day and night'. Someone asked a friend of mine once: 'Where do you worship?' He replied, 'I worship in Woolworth's, in the bank, in my car, in the supermarket … my life is a constant pageant of worship.' The person got the point.

Father, forgive me that I have been thinking of worship as something that only goes on at certain times or in certain seasons. Help me to worship You everywhere and in everything. Amen.

Worship, praise and thanksgiving

FOR READING AND MEDITATION
PSALM 22:1–11

'Yet you are enthroned as the Holy One; you are the praise of Israel.' (v.3)

All the biblical words for worship, whether in Hebrew or Greek, indicate an attitude of the heart or a posture of the body. It begins in the spiritual but also affects the physical. This is why devout Jews rock backwards and forwards when they pray; they see worship as both physical and spiritual. Praise, on the other hand, is generally related to the words of our mouths. When we come to thanksgiving we come again to the thought of utterance, the difference being this: we praise God for who He is, but we thank Him for what He does. Generally speaking, in worship we relate to God's holiness. In thanksgiving we relate to God's goodness. In praise we relate to God's greatness.

Father, may all these three aspects, worship, thanksgiving and praise, be present in my life not in a mechanical way but in a natural way. In Jesus' name. Amen.

'The joyful exchange'

FOR READING AND MEDITATION
LUKE 6:27–38

'Give, and it will be given to you.' (v.38)

Why does God ask us to worship Him? C.S. Lewis wrote: 'In commanding us to worship Him, God is inviting us to enjoy Him.' Because of the great respect God has for every human will, He will not force Himself upon us. He is, therefore, unable to give Himself to us until we first give ourselves to Him. The demand that God makes in insisting that we worship Him is not really a demand but an offer – an offer to share Himself with us in a personal way. God has in mind our enjoyment more than His own. When God asks us to worship Him, He is asking us to fulfil the deepest thing in Himself, which is His passionate desire to give Himself to us. Martin Luther called this 'the joyful exchange'.

Father, as I open the door of worship to give myself to You, You come through to give Yourself to me. This is truly a 'joyful exchange'. Amen.

The one thing

FOR READING AND MEDITATION
ISAIAH 43:14–28

'I am the LORD, your Holy One, Israel's Creator, your King.' (v.15)

What is the one thing above all others that true worshippers think of when approaching God? His almightiness? His goodness? His faithfulness? The answer is: His holiness! You have only to comb the Scriptures – particularly the Old Testament – to discover that those who were closest to the Lord thought more about His holiness than about any other attribute. I think it is true to say that this is one of the characteristics of God we think about least in our churches today. 'Holiness,' says J. Muilenburg, 'is the distinctive mark and signature of the divine. More than any other, the term "holiness" gives expression to the essential nature of the sacred.' Powerful words, because they point out that holiness is the way God is.

O Father, I too, like the worshipping seraphs, want to join in the refrain and say: Holy, holy, holy is the Lord Almighty. The whole earth is full of Your glory. Amen.

The divine emphasis

FOR READING AND MEDITATION
LEVITICUS 11:26–47

'I am the LORD ... your God; therefore be holy, because I am holy.' (v.45)

In the Scriptures, the holiness of God is emphasised more than any other aspect of God's nature. Theologians tell us that we ought not to think of divine holiness as just one of the attributes of God but as the essential ingredient of God. Because He is holy, all His attributes are holy. This is why, for example, theologians insist that whenever we talk about the love of God, we talk about it as holy love. If we remove holiness from God's love we can easily come out with mere sentimentalism. Stephen Charnock, says: 'His justice is a holy justice. His wisdom a holy wisdom. His arm of power "a holy arm" (Psa. 98:1) ... His name which signifies all attributes in conjunction is "holy" (Psa. 103:1).'

O Father, if ever Your Church needed a fresh vision of Your holiness it is today. Fill our pulpits with prophets and teachers who have a knowledge of the holy. Amen.

'The attribute of attributes'

FOR READING AND MEDITATION
REVELATION 4:1–11

'Holy, holy, holy is the Lord God Almighty, who was, and is, and is to come' (v.8)

The holiness of God is celebrated as no other attribute is celebrated before the throne of heaven. God Himself singles out this perfection to be honoured in a way that shows it to be, as John Howe put it: 'the attribute of attributes'. Emphasis in Hebrew (as in English) is sometimes conveyed by repeating a word twice. The word 'holy' is said not just twice but three times in our verse for today – the implication being that we are in the presence of something deep and profound. And indeed we are – the ineffable holiness of God. Is it not a fact that the more you make yourself aware of God's holiness in the Scriptures the more honour and respect you want to give Him?

O Lord my God, there is none like You in heaven above or in the earth beneath; glorious in holiness, mighty in splendour and wondrous in majesty. I worship You, my Father and my God. Amen.

Holiness is healthiness

FOR READING AND MEDITATION
2 CORINTHIANS 7:1–16

'… let us purify ourselves from everything that
contaminates body and spirit, perfecting holiness out of
reverence for God.' (v.1)

Over and over again in the Bible we are told: 'Be
holy even as I am holy.' We are not bidden to be
omnipotent or omniscient, but we are to be holy. This
is the prime way of honouring God. Are you seeking to
be the holy man or woman God wants you to be? God
has made holiness the moral condition necessary for the
health of His universe. Sin's temporary presence in the
world only accentuates this. Whatever is holy is healthy,
and evil is a moral sickness that must ultimately end in
death. The formation of the language itself suggests this,
the English word 'holy' deriving from the Anglo-Saxon
halig meaning 'well' or 'whole'. To be whole in Christian
terms means to be holy. To perfect holiness in our lives
is our goal.

*O Father, help me to focus first on my own moral health
and to be rid of all in my life that is contradictory to You
and Your holy nature. In Jesus' name I ask it. Amen.*

The divine X-ray

FOR READING AND MEDITATION
NUMBERS 17:1–13

*'The Israelites said to Moses, "We shall die! We are lost,
we are all lost!"' (v.12)*

The thing that strikes Isaiah as he stands in the
presence of God is not just the ineffable holiness
of God, but, by contrast, his own personal depravity
(Isa. 6:5). Up to this moment Isaiah probably thought
of himself as a good, upright, moral man. But here he
is face to face with the Holy One of Israel. Now Isaiah
is not being compared to the creatures whom God had
made; he is being compared to the Creator Himself, and
he sees himself as a man of unclean lips. The white light
of God's holiness acts like an X-ray that enables people
to see more clearly what is going on at the core of their
beings. If so, then how vital it is that sin-sick human
beings have an encounter with a holy God.

*O God, let the X-ray of Your holiness reveal the insidious
disease of sin that is deep within me. Make me more like
You, dear Lord. In Jesus' name. Amen.*

Invest now!

FOR READING AND MEDITATION
I PETER 1:3–25

'But just as he who called you is holy, so be holy in all you do …' (v.15)

How can we, like Isaiah, experience a personal encounter with God for ourselves? We can begin by looking at the nature of God's holiness as outlined in His Word. (These meditations I hope will have helped.) Then continue by waiting before God in fervent, believing prayer and inviting God to reveal Himself to you. This takes time of course, but any time spent with God is spiritual investment. Believe me, you will always get out more than you put in. But remember, a vision of God and His holiness will be emotionally overwhelming. It will cause you not only to cry out, 'Holy, holy, holy,' but also 'Woe is me, I am undone.'

O Father, I am afraid as I draw near, yet I draw near because I am afraid. Whatever sacrifice is needed in order to know You more, help me make it. In Jesus' name. Amen.

Amazing grace!

FOR READING AND MEDITATION
ROMANS 5:1–21

'But where sin increased, grace increased all the more ...'
(v.20)

E ven in the most noble people there is enough sin present to merit that person being consigned to eternal hell. Francis Schaeffer said: 'If God was to cut into any twenty-four hour period of my life, in the same way that a surgeon takes a biopsy, He would find sufficient evil within me to justify Him sending me to hell for ever.' We only understand sin when we see it set in the context of God's holiness. The more we understand sin the more we will understand divine grace. Larry Crabb says: 'When we have difficulty understanding God's grace it is only partly because we haven't experienced much grace in our lives. It is more because we haven't really gotten to the point where there is a desperate need for it.'

O Father, there is something in me that wants to protect myself from seeing that I am in a hopeless condition and desperate for grace. Help me see both my sin and Your grace more clearly. Amen.

Fearing for one's life!

FOR READING AND MEDITATION
NUMBERS 17:1–13

'Anyone who even comes near the tabernacle of the LORD will die.' (v.13)

When Isaiah saw the holiness of God he feared for his life. Anyone who saw God expected to die immediately. In fact, God said on one occasion: 'You cannot see my face, for no-one may see me and live' (Exod. 33:20). Perhaps now we can understand something of the concern that reverberated beneath Isaiah's words: 'My eyes have seen the King, the Lord Almighty.' His cry reflects much more than an ordinary conviction of sin: it reflects unspeakable horror. He needed no instruction from anyone about what might happen now. He had seen the King, the Lord Almighty. Now he must die! But does he? No, for as we shall see, God is not only a God of holiness – He is also the God of grace.

Father, help me see even more clearly the principle that is at work here, namely that before I can be saved I must admit I am lost and utterly helpless. Thank You for the salvation of grace. Amen.

'Surprised by joy!'

FOR READING AND MEDITATION
EPHESIANS 2:1–22

'For it is by grace you have been saved …' (v.8)

It isn't that God delights in striking fear into our hearts by the revelation of His holiness; it is just that being who He is, He cannot reveal Himself to us without this happening. But always His mercy and grace come to our aid to sustain us and cleanse us. Watch now as God moves towards Isaiah, not in judgment, but in grace. In the vision He inspires one of the seraphs to take a live coal from the altar, place it on the prophet's lips and declare: 'Your guilt is taken away and your sin atoned for.' Isaiah does not tell us what effect the seraph's action had on him. But if it was anything like the experience I had when God cleansed me, then Isaiah would have been, as C.S. Lewis put it, 'surprised by joy'.

Thank You, my Father, that I too have been 'surprised by joy'. When I expected to be consigned to hell, You showed me the way to heaven. Thank You for this revelation of Your grace. Amen.

Forgiven!

FOR READING AND MEDITATION
I PETER 2:11–25

'He himself bore our sins in his body on the tree ...' (v.24)

In Christian circles we talk so easily about forgiveness. But do we really understand what it cost God to forgive? David Seamands points out that forgiveness is always at great cost to the forgiving one. He says, 'When someone hurts us and we forgive them we take the hurt and indignation we feel and turn it back upon ourselves. Instead of putting it upon them we bear it in ourselves.' Forgiveness means taking your own pride, your own indignation, your own hurt, holding it to your heart and quenching it in the flame of your love. This is what God does with us when He forgives. Divine forgiveness is also costly. It cost God His only Son.

O God, nothing that anyone has done or can do against me compares to what I have done against You. Yet You have forgiven me. Help me now to forgive others, graciously. Amen.

An ounce of experience

FOR READING AND MEDITATION
GENESIS 22:1–19

'Some time later God tested Abraham. He said to him, "Abraham!" "Here I am," he replied.' (v.1)

There is an old saying: 'An ounce of experience is worth a ton of theory.' I can almost guarantee that the person who influenced you to come to Christ was himself or herself someone who had experienced the grace of God. The implication in Isaiah 6:8 behind the words: 'Who will go for us?' is that the task on earth has to be done by the men and women on earth. Isaiah didn't hesitate. What about you? Is God calling you to some task and you feel hesitant and uncertain? Perhaps it is because you have not had a powerful enough vision of the Lord. Those who see Him – really see Him – cannot help but say 'Here am I. Send me'.

O God, day by day I am seeing more of Your glory. Help me say in response to whatever You are calling me to do: 'Here am I. Send me!' Amen.

'The strange predicament of God'

FOR READING AND MEDITATION
JEREMIAH 26:1–16

'The LORD sent me to prophesy against this house and this city …' (v.12)

S omeone has described the Almighty asking help of human beings as 'the strange predicament of God'. The Almighty God, who holds the world in the hollow of His hand, seeks to enlist our support in the relaying of His truth to the men and women of this planet. It isn't because God is powerless that He asks our help. He chooses to do so because that is His way. He wants us to be involved with Him in redeeming the world. John Wesley is reported to have said: 'God does nothing in the world redemptively except through prayer.' God wants it to be a team effort. 'Who will go?' Does that mean that if you and I do not make ourselves available to Him then some things just might not get done? I wonder.

Father, it humbles me to think that You want me on Your team. I am overwhelmed by the invitation, but my heart cries out 'Yes, yes, yes!' Use me today. Amen.

A call to failure!

FOR READING AND MEDITATION
JEREMIAH 5:18–31

'Hear this ... who have eyes but do not see, who have ears but do not hear ...' (v.21)

God clearly tells Isaiah that his message will have the ironic but justly deserved effect of hardening the callous hearts of the rebellious Israelites, thus rendering the warnings of judgment sure (Isa. 6:9–10). What a depressing commission. This is none other than a call to failure! How do you think Isaiah and other prophets felt about the fact that after offering themselves as a messenger of God they are told that the message will have a hardening rather than a softening effect? Whatever Isaiah felt, we know one thing for sure – he set out to faithfully preach the word he had been given, clearly believing that it was not up to him to understand, but to stand; not to reason, but to obey.

O God, I am Your disciple, but sometimes I am afraid to follow where You lead me. Help me do Your bidding, whatever the outcome. In Jesus' name. Amen.

No excuse

FOR READING AND MEDITATION
MATTHEW 13:1–17

'You will be ever hearing but never understanding; you will be ever seeing but never perceiving.' (v.14)

The gospel heard and accepted is life; the gospel heard and refused is death. As Dr Martyn Lloyd-Jones puts it: 'The same sun that melts ice, hardens clay.' Now, it is important to realise that neither God in Isaiah 6:9 nor Jesus in the passage before us is saying that some hearers would not understand but, rather, that those who are not willing to hear the word of the Lord will find the truth hidden from them. But why preach the gospel to those who will not receive it? It is to expose and highlight their hard-hearted resistance in such a way that no one will be able to say they did not hear, and so that they will be absolutely without excuse when judgment comes.

O Father, I see even more clearly that Your Word is not only a saving word but a searing word; it heals but also hardens. Amen.

One ray of hope

FOR READING AND MEDITATION
JOB 14:1–12

'... there is hope for a tree: If it is cut down, it will sprout again ...' (v.7)

At the end of Isaiah 6, the prophet is going to witness Israel becoming like a wasteland. He has a long, hard job ahead of him, prophesying to a people who, in the main, just do not want to hear. However, there is one ray of hope, which we see in the last phrase of the chapter. The Living Bible puts it most effectively: 'Yet a tenth – a remnant – will survive; and though Israel is invaded again and again and destroyed, yet Israel will be like a tree cut down, whose stump still lives to grow again.' When would the people listen? Only after they had come to the end and had nowhere to turn but to God. Will we, like Israel, pursue our own paths and come back to Him only when we have nowhere left to turn?

O Father, when will I learn that Your way is the only sure way. Forgive me for the times when I prefer my way to Your way. May I put Your interests before self-interest. In Jesus' name. Amen.

Enjoying majority status!

FOR READING AND MEDITATION
ROMANS 11:1–12

'So too, at the present time there is a remnant chosen by grace.' (v.5)

True spirituality was a minority thing in Old Testament times, and true spirituality is a minority thing in New Testament times. I am not an alarmist, but I do see a parallel between Isaiah's day and the day in which we live. What a state we are in at present – and things are destined to get worse. But God has His remnant in this age as He has had in every age. If you are a committed follower of Jesus Christ then you are part of that remnant. And God has always used a redeemed remnant to change the world. You and I may be in the minority as far as the world is concerned, but as someone once put it 'one person with God is in the majority'. We are minorities with a majority status! Hallelujah!

Father, I am so thankful that I am part of today's remnant, but I am even more thankful that that remnant is part of You. By myself I am nothing, but with You I am a majority. Amen.

The church at Antioch

FOR READING AND MEDITATION
ACTS 11:1–21

'… they … praised God, saying, "So then, God has even granted the Gentiles repentance unto life."' (v.18)

The church at Jerusalem never quite got over being Jewish. While Jewish history was clearly an essential prelude to New Testament Christianity, some of the Jewish Christians in Jerusalem failed to sense what God was really doing in forming a single new humanity in Christ, and for a while hindered rather than helped the growth of the Church. Go through the account of the church at Antioch with a fine-toothed comb, and you will not find one single thing that was marginal or trivial. Everything that happened at Antioch had destiny in it. The springboard from which the gospel was launched into Europe was Antioch and, as Christians, we have an exciting personal reason to be grateful for that.

Father, as You touched the hearts of Your early disciples to share with others, touch my heart in the same way today. Amen.

The first mark

FOR READING AND MEDITATION
ACTS 11:22–30

*'It was at Antioch … that the disciples were first called
"Christians".' (v.26, Moffatt)*

Now we come to the first mark of a Christian church
– the Christians at Antioch *embodied the spirit of
the everlasting Christ*. It was not a matter of chance that it
was there that the disciples were first called 'Christians'.
The name was not just a label, for in those days names
were given in order to identify a characteristic. If a
characteristic changed, the name changed. Barnabas,
the last of a large family, was called at one time 'Joseph',
meaning 'one more'. So effective was his ministry
that they called him 'Barnabas', which means 'Son of
Encouragement'. When people saw how the disciples
at Antioch lived their daily lives, they could see but one
characteristic – the spirit of Christ. Thus there was only
one name they could give them – Christians.

*Lord Jesus, thank You for reminding me that Your
characteristics can live in Your children. Let them live in me,
and in all of us who form Your redeemed society. Amen.*

MARCH 3

Glance at men – gaze at Jesus

FOR READING AND MEDITATION
1 CORINTHIANS 3:1–7

'For when one says, "I follow Paul," and another, "I follow Apollos," are you not mere men?' (v.4)

The church at Corinth started doing something that has plagued Christianity ever since – they began to focus their primary allegiance not on Christ, but on those who ministered to them in His name. Paul broke the links of loyalty to men and fastened them on Christ. He was saying in essence: glance at men but gaze on Christ. The present-day Church is not Christian enough. God may not want to take us out of our denominations, but He does want to take the denomination out of us. It is not our denominations that God is against, but denominationalism – the spirit that puts the denomination ahead of Christ. When the world sees us putting more emphasis on Christ, things will begin to happen.

Gracious Father, forgive us for the way we have fragmented Your image before the eyes of the world by our divisions and petty squabbles. Help us to mirror a true reflection of Christ. Amen.

Good news – not good views

FOR READING AND MEDITATION
ACTS 8:26–40

*'Then Philip began with that very passage of Scripture
and told him the good news about Jesus.' (v.35)*

The supreme emphasis of the Church must be on
Christ. Throughout Church history, every rediscovery
and re-emphasis on Jesus has brought renewal and
revival, while every departure from Him has brought
decay. When the persecuted disciples left Jerusalem
and came to Antioch, they began at once to preach,
not 'the good views about Jesus Christ', but 'the good
news of Jesus Christ'. If God and Christ are left out of the
Church's emphasis, we have nothing left but humanism.
Acts 11:20–21 would then read: 'They preached good
views about the good life; the weak hand of humanism
was upon them and nobody turned to the Lord.' The
church at Antioch had Jesus as its central theme, and
so must we.

*O Father, help us – Your people – to make You both the
centre and the circumference of our individual and
corporate activities. Forgive us that we have not been
Christian enough. Amen.*

Raising the percentage

FOR READING AND MEDITATION
JOHN 12:20–36

'But I, when I am lifted up from the earth, will draw all men to myself.' (v.32)

A young university student said: 'I am 100% for Christ, but only 50% for the Church.' One of the tragedies of today's Church is that some are preaching the principles of Christ and missing the Person. This leads people to say, 'I will live by Christian principles without coming into a close personal relationship with Jesus.' The Christian life then becomes a tense striving to live by principles, instead of a trustful fellowship with a Person. Make no mistake about it, if today's Church loses the Person of Jesus, it loses God as well. The result is a barren humanism. If the Church does not make Christ central, it ceases to justify its existence.

O Father, save us from preaching just mere principles and missing the reality of Jesus Christ. Help us to lift Jesus higher. Amen.

The true *koinonia*

FOR READING AND MEDITATION
ACTS 11:26

'For a whole year they … were guests of the church …'
(v.26, Amp)

The second characteristic of a Christian church is *a strong sense of being a corporate body.* Paul and Barnabas, we read, were 'guests of the church' at Antioch for a whole year. The church at Antioch was not just a collection of worshipping individuals, but a corporate body – 'an organism of the Holy Spirit'. Those who have studied the impact of Christianity on the first-century world tell us that the thing that won people to Christ was not only the message – important though that was – but also the unity, love and strong sense of the corporate that those early Christians possessed. Non-Christians were deeply impressed with this 'undecaying' society in the midst of a decaying society and, because of this, gave attention to their message.

Father, instil once again into Your Church the same sense of unity, love and togetherness that pervaded the church at Antioch. Give us the sense of being a body – Your Body. Amen.

Corporate living

FOR READING AND MEDITATION
HEBREWS 10:19–39

*'Let us not give up meeting together ... but let us
encourage one another ...' (v.25)*

Many Christians look upon life in Christ as an
individual thing. Almost every schoolboy knows
these days that a cancer cell is one that demands to be
ministered to instead of ministering to the rest of the body.
It is therefore cancerous instead of being contributive.
The idea that you can be a solitary Christian without
relating to others in the Body of Christ is false. Over the
years I have watched some come into the Church who
refuse to recognise the importance of their corporate
relationship or develop close relationships with other
believers. Inevitably the fire of their faith begins to die
down. The famous preacher D.L. Moody used to say: 'No
corporate life; no Christian life.'

*O Father, help me not to be a cancerous cell in Your
Body, but a contributive one. Teach me not just to live
in fellowship with my fellow believers, but to enjoy it. In
Jesus' name. Amen.*

Christ's influence

FOR READING AND MEDITATION
LUKE 4:14–30

'The Spirit of the Lord is on me, because he has anointed me …' (v.18)

Many churches lack the reality of what the Early Church called the *koinonia* – deep or close fellowship. Many are just groups of individuals who touch elbows on Sundays and then return to their isolated individualism for the rest of the week. Someone has suggested that the history of human relationships might be summed up as five stages: (1) owner and slave; (2) master and servant; (3) employer and employee; (4) comrades and dissidents; (5) brothers and sisters. Christ's coming marked the beginning of great changes in the world of relationships. It took a long time, perhaps, for slavery to be abolished, but it was through the Church's influence that it was finally brought to an end.

My Father and my God, I am so grateful that You have put such an infinite worth on every one of us that You sent Your Son to set us free from every chain of bondage. Amen.

The world's struggle with a word

FOR READING AND MEDITATION
HEBREWS 13:1–16

'Continue to love each other with true brotherly love.'
(v.1, TLB)

Coleridge said: 'The world is struggling with words – words which express relationships.' We have seen the struggle with the words owner, slave, master, servant, employer, employee, comrade, dissident. At each stage there is an attempt to get to an ultimate basis of relationship. How refreshing it is to turn from a world struggling with words to the Christian Church, where we are introduced to each other, not as slaves, employees or comrades, but as brothers and sisters in Christ. This is the ultimate word in relationships. When we recognise the filial relationship that exists between those of us who are Christ's redeemed people, and act on it, then the Church will be more of a family and less of a feud.

Father, I am so thankful when I see that while the world is struggling to find a word – I have it. Help us to come into the reality of what we are – the family of God. In Jesus' name. Amen.

'Organs one of another'

FOR READING AND MEDITATION
EPHESIANS 4:17–32

'… we are organs one of another.' (v.25, literal translation from the Greek)

Once we recognise that the Church is a corporate Body, then we must obey the underlying law of corporate living. And what is that? A literal translation of Ephesians 4:25 puts it like this: 'For we are organs one of another.' The biggest single evil in corporate relationships is jealousy. If a member of your church excels in something, say in preaching or teaching, then he or she becomes the organ of ministry for you. You should rejoice that the organ is functioning. The strength of one is the strength of all. God has linked us together as organs of one Body, so that as we function together and in harmony with one another, we build up the Church and help make it a strong and vigorous ministry in the world.

Father, let the wonder of this truth – that we are organs one of another – take hold of me in a way that will transform my outlook and my relationships in Your Body. Amen.

A classless society

FOR READING AND MEDITATION
2 PETER 1:1–11

'To those who through the righteousness of our God and Saviour Jesus Christ have received a faith as precious as ours.' (v.1)

The next mark of a Christian church is that *it is a place where people of different backgrounds and ministries are held together in unbroken fellowship.* 'Among the prophets and teachers of the church at Antioch were … Symeon (also called "the black man") … Manaen (the foster-brother of King Herod)' (Acts 13:1, TLB). These two men represent a difference in class; Symeon (Simeon, NIV) came from the lower social class and Manaen from the upper class. Evidently, all class distinction was wiped out, and each person was valued as one for whom Christ had died. The Christian society, when true to itself, is a society of the sons and daughters of God. Is there class in a real home? How can there be? Love is equal and equalising.

Lord Jesus, You whose love is all-embracing, pour into my heart this day that selfsame love, so that I might love all – and love all equally. Amen.

'A foreign substance'

FOR READING AND MEDITATION
GALATIANS 3:15–29

'There is neither Jew nor Greek, slave nor free, male nor female, for you are all one in Christ Jesus.' (v.28)

The church at Antioch held together men who were of a different social class and men of different race. In Acts 13:1–3, Simeon, called Niger (black), along with others, laid hands on Barnabas and Paul to send them to preach the gospel to white Europe. The comment is made as if nothing extraordinary had happened. To treat a man on the basis of his colour is to introduce into the Body of Christ a foreign substance that will, in time, poison it. The Church must return to the spirit that prevailed at Antioch. Though this matter of overcoming racial prejudice is not easy, it must be done. I know the diehards will die hard and with protest, but die they must; the Church is a 'raceless' society.

O Father, may I be class-blind and colour-blind. I don't want to be one who introduces a foreign substance into Your Body. For Jesus' sake. Amen.

Body ministry

FOR READING AND MEDITATION
EPHESIANS 4:7–16

'It was he who gave some to be apostles, some to be prophets, some to be evangelists, and some to be pastors and teachers.' (v.11)

We read that in the church at Antioch, there were 'prophets and teachers'. Broadly speaking, a teacher is one who draws from the past and brings out of revealed truth 'treasures new and old'. A prophet is one whose gaze is set on the future, and who constantly prods the Church to lay hold on the promises of God. Both are necessary, and both are equally important. The Church must not allow these two ministries – or any other ministry – to produce a cleavage in the community. At Antioch, these two ministries each contributed to the healthy functioning of the whole. Happy is the church where any one ministry is not given priority above another, but all are seen as vital to the growth of the entire Body.

Father, I see so clearly that many ministries are needed to build up Your Body. Forgive us that we sometimes prefer one above another. Help us to rejoice in every ministry. Amen.

Amazing grace!

FOR READING AND MEDITATION
EPHESIANS 4:1–7

'But to each one of us grace was given according to the measure of Christ's gift.' (v.7, NASB)

P aul and Barnabas parted, we are told in Acts 15:39, because of a 'sharp disagreement' (Amp). Here was a good opportunity for two denominations to emerge – the Barnabites, who believed the Church should be redemptive, and the Paulites, who believed the Church should be kept pure. But the church at Antioch held together these two strong men who differed. Although they parted 'in irritation' (Moffatt), with Barnabas taking John Mark and Paul taking Silas, they were both 'commended … to the grace of the Lord' by the church. They parted, but they both came back to Antioch, their spiritual home – held together, in spite of their differences, through the prayerful concern of the church.

Father, give me growing confidence in the power of Your transforming grace. Show me how to commit such difficult issues to the limitless and unfailing power of Your grace. Amen.

'For His sake'

FOR READING AND MEDITATION
COLOSSIANS 3:1–17

'And whatever you do, whether in word or deed, do it all in the name of the Lord Jesus ...' (v.17)

The Christians at Antioch fell back on the principle that in everything they must act in accordance with the spirit of Christ. They were held together around the Person of Christ. No church will go far wrong, even though it may lack experienced and competent leadership, if it has a consuming desire to put Christ first in all matters. No human being, custom or idea can hold a church together for long; only divine shoulders can bear that responsibility. Barnabas and Paul were still one despite their differences, for they were dedicated to Christ and held together in Him. And the church that holds together in Him will inevitably hold together strong men and women who differ.

O Father, make us one. Gather us up in spite of our differences. Help us to see that when we are dedicated to You, no differences can drive us apart. Amen.

'The society of the caring'

FOR READING AND MEDITATION
I CORINTHIANS 12:12–27

*'That there should be no division in the body, but that
the members should have the same care for one another.'
(v.25, NASB)*

The next mark of a Christian church that we shall examine is that of caring. The believers in Antioch were *a group of people who cared*. When the prophet Agabus predicted that a severe famine was imminent, the Christians at Antioch resolved at once to send relief to their brothers and sisters in Jerusalem. This was an extremely important moment. If they had simply sent a letter to the church in Jerusalem assuring them of their prayers, they might have fixed the attitude of future generations of Christians to economic problems. Our faith would then have become mere idealism. Fortunately their reaction was not one of idealism, but realism. A church that doesn't care is a church on its way to oblivion.

Father, help me to take my place in the community in which You have placed me as one who cares – really cares. For Jesus' sake. Amen.

Caring – a top priority

FOR READING AND MEDITATION
GALATIANS 6:1–10

'… let us do good to all men, and especially to those who are of the household of faith.' (v.10, RSV)

Why is the ministry of caring such an important part of the Christian Church? Because God cares – and has called us to be His messengers of care, first to each other and then to the world. I used to think that a Christian's first priority was to care for those outside the Church, and then, if there was enough energy left, for those inside the Church. I have grown, however, to see the wisdom of putting the emphasis where Scripture puts it. When unbelievers see the concern and interest we show in caring for one another, our outreach to the world will come across with a far greater impact. As our words flow out of a lifestyle of caring, our message will penetrate their defences and work with greater power.

Father, I see that it is not so much what we say, but what we are, that is so important. Help us to be Your messengers and ministers of care. For Jesus' sake. Amen.

Caring begins in the Body

FOR READING AND MEDITATION
2 CORINTHIANS 7:1–12

'… but that our care for you in the sight of God might
appear unto you.' (v.12, AV)

I once counselled a minister who came to me feeling
pretty shattered because of something that had
happened in his community. Apparently one of his
church members had invited the receptionist at the
local health centre to come to his church, and she had
responded something like this: 'I know most of the
members of your church, and many of them come here
regularly for their supplies of antidepressants or nerve
pills to cope with their psychosomatic problems. When
you can show me you have something in your church
that can help people with their personal needs, then I
might consider responding to your invitation.' It is not
enough to say to each other that God cares – we must
take steps to show that we care too.

O God, help me to link myself to Your plans and purposes
so that I make the greatest possible contribution to the part
of Your Body in which You have placed me. In Jesus' name.
Amen.

Becoming contributive people

FOR READING AND MEDITATION
1 JOHN 3:11–24

'If anyone has material possessions and sees his brother in need but has no pity on him, how can the love of God be in him?' (v.17)

Paul says: 'If a man will not work, he shall not eat' (2 Thess. 3:10). This verse refers, not to someone who cannot work because of redundancy, unemployment or sickness, but to someone who is able to work but does not want to. If he is not willing to contribute, says the apostle, then let him starve. Strong words! You can give to people according to their need out of sympathy and pity, but to inspire people to give back to others according to their ability after their own needs are met requires a strength of character that human nature, apart from God's grace, is not able to achieve. It takes the Holy Spirit working in our lives to make us contributive people, not just people who give contributions to others.

Father, I see so clearly that only You can give me the character that cries, not 'Give to me!', but 'How can I give to others?' Take away everything that hinders my growth in this area. Amen.

The uniqueness of Christian caring

FOR READING AND MEDITATION
PHILIPPIANS 2:1–11

'Let Christ Himself be your example as to what your attitude should be.' (v.5, Phillips)

The God we see in the Scriptures is a God who cares – cares enough to give Himself on a cross. That is the ultimate in caring. The wonderful thing, of course, is this – the Church, because it came out of God, is uniquely structured for caring. This is not to denigrate the excellent work done by the secular caring professions, but the Church has a unique contribution to make in this area, in that it cares, not just for physical needs, but for spiritual needs also. A society that cares only for physical needs is only half caring. A society that cares only for spiritual needs is only half caring. The Church must care for every human need, for a reduced caring is really a cancelled caring.

O Father, give me a transfusion of Your loving care and concern. Put within my withered veins the life that reaches out to others who are in need. Let the transfusion begin – today. Amen.

How Saul became Paul

FOR READING AND MEDITATION
GALATIANS 1:11–24

'For even before I was born God had chosen me to be his, and called me … to reveal his Son within me …'
(vv.15–16, TLB)

The church at Antioch had the right climate in which those with special abilities could be prepared for leadership. After spending a short time at Antioch, Barnabas came to an important conclusion. He said to himself: 'This is the kind of church I would like Saul of Tarsus to see.' Barnabas brought Saul out of comparative isolation in Tarsus into the mainstream of Christian life and action in Antioch. His trip to Tarsus was one of the greatest things Barnabas did, for in introducing Saul to Antioch, he brought the young disciple into an atmosphere that greatly contributed to his spiritual development. It was after being at Antioch that Saul became known as Paul. Antioch not only welcomed him; it made him.

O Father, thank You for the power that lies within Your Church to change and transform people. May the power that throbbed in the church at Antioch be in my church – this very weekend. Amen.

'A seed happening'

FOR READING AND MEDITATION
PSALM 37:1–40

'The steps of a man are from the LORD, and he establishes him in whose way he delights.' (v.23, RSV)

Barnabas bringing Saul to Antioch was a seed happening – a seed that produced one of the greatest spiritual harvests in the world's history. The church in which we fellowship can either make us or break us, develop us or demean us. We should pray much about the church to which we attach ourselves, and need to be sure that in joining it we are following divine leading. I emphasise yet again: it was the Holy Spirit working through the church at Antioch that made Saul into Paul. The lessons he had learned while closeted with the Lord in isolation now needed to be worked out in a more public situation. The best preparation for spiritual leadership is to be in a local church where the grace of God is flowing.

O God, help me sense Your direction and leading in my life as did Your servant Barnabas. If You have any word to speak to me this day, help me to hear that word – and follow it. Amen.

The power of grace

FOR READING AND MEDITATION
ACTS 20:17–38

'And now I commend you to God and to the word of His grace, which is able to build you up ...' (v.32, NASB)

The name 'Saul' means 'demanded', while the name 'Paul' means 'the little one'. The change of name indicates something of the inner change that went on in Saul's life during his sojourn in Antioch. Saul, prior to his conversion, most certainly lived up to his name. He 'demanded' everything for himself, even the lives of those who professed to follow Jesus of Nazareth. But what a change took place in him as he adopted Christian principles and applied them in his life. 'The grace of God', as D.L. Moody said, 'is the soil out of which all great service for God grows and develops.' A church where God's grace flows abundantly will be a church that has the potential for producing productive and powerful Christians.

O God, how can I ever sufficiently thank You for the gift of Your grace? Help me to understand and to live in its awesome power. Amen.

Not attainment – but obtainment

FOR READING AND MEDITATION
MATTHEW 5:1–16

'Blessed are the poor in spirit, for theirs is the kingdom of heaven.' (v.3)

The word 'grace' means 'unmerited favour'. When we become poor enough to receive, to be receptive, the kingdom of heaven and all its resources will belong to us. Perhaps during the days spent at Antioch, Saul learned in a new way the truth that the Christian life is not a matter of attainment, but obtainment. Saul the 'demander' became Paul, 'the little one', by becoming poor enough to receive. I have often used this phrase in my writing and I do not hesitate to use it again here: 'The Christian life is not our responsibility, but our response to His ability.' Antioch taught Paul receptivity – receptivity to grace. So Antioch made Paul by making him receptive.

Father, help me to realise that I am so rich in grace that I can afford to give some of it away to others. In Jesus' name. Amen.

'By the grace of God'

FOR READING AND MEDITATION
I CORINTHIANS 15:1–11

'But by the grace of God I am what I am ...' (v.10)

When we understand that we live by grace – the unmerited favour of God – and that our achievements and accomplishments are all due to that, pride is levelled and true humility shines forth from our lives. Nothing is more wonderful than to fellowship in a church where everyone realises that they are what they are by God's grace. In such an atmosphere, Sauls can be turned into Pauls; those who are caught up in the inconsequential can be turned in the direction of a national, even a worldwide ministry. Is your church like that? Well, it can be – provided all concerned lay hold on the truth that we are what we are, not by merit or by achievement, but by the undeserved, unfailing, unlimited grace of God.

Father, let the wonder and meaning of Your grace permeate every cell of my being. And, from this day forward, let me rejoice, not in my achievements for You, but Your achievements through me. Amen.

No cost – no contribution

FOR READING AND MEDITATION
ROMANS 8:12–28

'… if indeed we share in his sufferings in order that we
may also share in his glory.' (v.17)

The next mark of a Christian church is *suffering* – or,
if you prefer, *the mark of the cross*. We read: 'Those
who had been scattered by the trouble which arose
over Stephen, made their way as far as … Antioch'
(Acts 11:19, Moffatt). Following the death of Stephen,
fierce persecution arose against the church in Jerusalem,
causing many of them to be scattered to different
towns and cities. The Christians, however, did not go
underground, but overland – they 'went everywhere
preaching the word' (Acts 8:4, AV). The mark of the
cross was not only built into the foundation of the
church at Antioch, it was there too in its day-to-day
functioning. It cost the believers at Antioch something
to be Christians.

*O Father, I confess I am but a frail human being and tend
to draw back from anything to do with pain and suffering.
Build in me over these next few days the mark of the cross.
Amen.*

Needed grace for needed moments

FOR READING AND MEDITATION
LUKE 12:35–53

'But I have a baptism to undergo, and how distressed I am until it is accomplished!' (v.50, NASB)

J esus said: 'Remember the words I spoke to you: "No servant is greater than his master." If they persecuted me, they will persecute you' (John 15:20). I know many Christians who, when they come up against this and similar passages, quickly flip over the pages of their Bible and focus on more appealing texts. Permit me to share something with you that may sound direct and challenging but is nevertheless an important fact – nothing can ever be gained by avoiding reality. One thing is sure, however – God will never allow us to endure anything for Him without at the same time providing the needed strength and grace. We can rely, as someone put it, on 'needed grace for needed moments'.

Blessed Lord Jesus, as I think of Your own personal suffering that awful night prior to the cross, I am so grateful that the same grace that enabled You is also available to me. Amen.

The three who bore crosses

FOR READING AND MEDITATION
JOHN 12:20–36

'… it was for this very reason I came to this hour.' (v.27)

We pause now to ask ourselves a challenging question: Is suffering for Christ something I must have thrust upon me, or is it something I will choose? On that day at Golgotha, there were three who bore crosses. Neither of the thieves who died alongside Christ had any say in the way they suffered; it was something that was thrust upon them by the might of Rome. The cross of Jesus, however, was a cross He chose for Himself. He put Himself in such deep contact with men that the cross became inevitable, but behind it lay a personal choice. That is the highest attitude of all. Since the world is bound to nail you to a cross once you become a follower of Jesus Christ, it is better to anticipate it, to accept it and make it redemptive, than to try to avoid it.

Father, thank You for reminding me that the cross of Jesus is not an isolated thing – it continues in us. Help me to wear the honour of being a cross-bearer with joy and distinction. Amen.

'Nothing in us to hate'

FOR READING AND MEDITATION
HEBREWS 13:1–16

'… let us go out to Him outside the camp, bearing His reproach.' (v.13, NASB)

Generally speaking, the Church today is seldom bold to rebuke sin and corruption – whether in church or political circles – and we pass over glaring biblical violations just in case anyone should become offended. We are respectable, considerate, accommodating, understanding, polite – and ineffective. John Stott, the well-known Anglican leader, asked in one of his sermons: 'Why is it that Christians here in Britain do not suffer much? The ugly truth is that we tend to avoid suffering by compromise. Our moral standards are often not noticeably higher than the world's … our lives do not challenge or rebuke unbelievers by their integrity or purity or love. The world sees nothing in us to hate.'

Father, Your Church is not the force it ought to be in our society. Give us repentant hearts so that we shall break with all compromise and rise to new heights of strength and power. Amen.

He is risen!

FOR READING AND MEDITATION
PHILIPPIANS 3:1–14

*'That I may know Him, and the power of His resurrection
…' (v.10, NASB)*

We have been saying over the past few days that
the mark of the cross was on the church at
Antioch – it was established by men and women who
were prepared to suffer for their faith. And because the
mark of the cross was on it, so also was the mark of the
resurrection, for you cannot have one without the other.
We must not, however, depend solely on the historical
fact of the resurrection, but on the resurrected Christ.
And not just on a resurrected Christ of the past, but on
the actual, living Christ through whom and in whom
we meet God now. Related to this living Christ, nothing
ought ever to dismay us or make us afraid because we
can know the power of His resurrection for ourselves.

*Lord, help me to lay hold afresh on the fact that nothing
can defeat me, since nothing defeated You. Implant that
thought so deeply in my heart that it will control my whole
life. Amen.*

The voice of encouragement

FOR READING AND MEDITATION
HEBREWS 3:1–14

'But encourage one another daily ... so that none of you may be hardened by sin's deceitfulness.' (v.13)

Another element that went into the making of the church at Antioch was *the ministry of encouragement*. We read that when Barnabas arrived in Antioch, he 'encouraged them all to remain true to the Lord with all their hearts' (Acts 11:23). Barnabas was known in the Early Church as 'the Great Encourager'. It's interesting to note that it was only after Barnabas had vouched for Saul that the latter was accepted by the apostles (Acts 9:27–28). What an influential man Barnabas appears to have been. It is no surprise, therefore, to discover that when the apostles decided to send someone to help the newly-formed Christian church in Antioch, they chose Barnabas – the Great Encourager! Could that same title be applied to you?

Father, may I too become a great encourager. Take me and prune from my heart all the words and ways of discouragement and replace them with an encouraging spirit. Amen.

'Coming alongside'

FOR READING AND MEDITATION
HEBREWS 10:1–25

'... let us consider how to stimulate one another to love and good deeds.' (v.24, NASB)

W hat precisely is 'encouragement'? The meaning can best be seen in the related Greek word *parakletos*, which means 'one who comes alongside to help'. The same word is used in John 15 to describe the Holy Spirit – 'Comforter'. Just think of it – we come closest to the work and ministry of the Holy Spirit when we are involved in the ministry of encouragement. Many Christians believe going to church is simply a matter of sitting in their seats, singing a few hymns and listening to a sermon. But that is only a part of it. When we meet other Christians we should not keep a distance but come alongside to encourage them, spur them on, stimulate and affirm them.

Father, help me to 'come alongside' people in need. Make me sensitive without being intrusive, and give me the insights and words that I need to encourage one of Your children. Amen.

'Every Christian can do it'

FOR READING AND MEDITATION
2 CHRONICLES 35:1–16

'He appointed the priests to their duties and encouraged them in the service of the LORD's temple.' (v.2)

William Barclay, in his exposition of the book of Hebrews, says, 'One of the highest of human duties is the duty of encouragement. It is easy to pour cold water on people's enthusiasm; it is easy to discourage others. We have a Christian duty to encourage one another. Many a time, a word of praise or thanks or appreciation or cheer has kept a man on his feet.' The most wonderful thing about encouragement is this – every Christian can do it. You don't need to have studied at Bible college or to possess a degree in theology; it can be practised by any member of Christ's Body at any time and anywhere.

O God, help me to approach this whole issue of encouragement in a spirit of humility, so that I can be at my best – Your best – in encouraging others. For Jesus' sake. Amen.

Appreciation and affirmation

FOR READING AND MEDITATION
ACTS 15:22–33

'The people read it and were glad for its encouraging message.' (v.31)

There is far more to encouragement than a smile and a quick pat on the back; encouragement is a ministry, which, as Hebrews says, we must concentrate on and think through carefully: 'Let us consider how to stimulate one another.' There are two thoughts contained in the word 'encouragement' – one is appreciation and the other affirmation. When we appreciate someone, we express praise for what they have done, but when we affirm someone, our words affirm not so much what they have done, but who they are. Appreciation comes and goes because it is usually linked to a person's accomplishments; affirmation is much deeper, because it is directed towards the person himself.

O Father, help me to be so in touch with You that I can be a great encourager of others. For Jesus' sake. Amen.

Encouragement encourages

FOR READING AND MEDITATION
I THESSALONIANS 5:1–11

'Therefore encourage one another and build each other up, just as in fact you are doing.' (v.11)

Romans 12:8 states that some people are specially gifted to develop their financial resources and give large amounts to God's work. Those who are not gifted in this way are not excused from giving however, for all are expected to give to the work of God irrespective of whether they are specially gifted or not. Similarly some are specially gifted to encourage. The gifted givers play a special part in the Body of Christ, just as do the gifted encouragers. Although Scripture recognises that some have a special ability to encourage, that does not exclude us from the responsibility of learning the art of encouragement. Encouragement encourages others to become encouragers.

My Lord and my God, help me to show and share encouragement with everyone I meet today. You have encouraged me – now let me encourage others. For Jesus' sake. Amen.

'Every generation needs regeneration'

FOR READING AND MEDITATION
MATTHEW 18:1–14

'... unless you are converted and become as little children, you will by no means enter the kingdom of heaven.' (v.3, NKJV)

Another crucial element in the life of the church at Antioch was *evangelism* (Acts 11:21). Any church that doesn't set out to convert people is sub-Christian, no matter how often it names the name of Christ. As someone put it: 'Every generation needs regeneration.' When the church at Antioch focused on introducing others to the gospel of the Lord Jesus Christ, it fulfilled one of its highest and most vital functions. Without that fulfilment, it would itself have remained unfulfilled. A church historian has said: 'If the church at Antioch had fulfilled all other things and had left out evangelism, its heart would have ceased to beat. It would have been a body without a heartbeat – a corpse.'

O Father, who can look into Your face and not want to share what they have seen? As a Christian I am inherently an evangelist. Help me not to choke that impulse. In Jesus' name I ask it. Amen.

'Convert me, or I'll sue you'

FOR READING AND MEDITATION
MATTHEW 23:15

*'You travel over land and sea to win a single convert,
and … make him twice as much a son of hell as you are.'*
(v.15, NKJV)

Jesus saw to the heart of proselytism and knew it to be nothing more than a corporate egotism that wanted to add to collective power and prestige by numbers. Instead, Jesus insisted on conversion. Conversion is a profound change in character – not just a change of label. It is the Church's business to focus on the need for conversion, and when it does not do so, or feels it can no longer do so, it has no right to be called a Christian church. People are flocking to the churches that can and do convert them, and are deserting the churches that cannot. In an evangelistic service, a man sent up a note to the evangelist which read: 'Convert me – or I'll sue you for breach of promise.'

O Father, with all my heart I cry out today – help me to help others to see You. When I speak haltingly, perhaps then You will speak most clearly. Amen.

All expression deepens impression

FOR READING AND MEDITATION
MATTHEW 10:1–15

'Freely you have received, freely give.' (v.8)

Many years ago, when the Constitution of India was being debated, the question of 'the right to profess, practise and propagate one's faith' was brought up. Many Indians objected to the word 'propagate' until one wise old man said: 'To propagate one's faith is an integral part of the Christian heritage, so if you do not give the Christians the right to propagate, you do not give them the right to practise. They cannot profess and practise if they do not propagate.' Expression deepens impression, and that which is not expressed begins to die. In sharing the gospel an amazing law of the personality comes into action – the more we share, the more gripped we are by what we share.

O Father, help me to make good use of this law of the personality. Freely I have received, so freely will I give. Henceforth this shall be my motive and motto in all things. Amen.

Twice born

FOR READING AND MEDITATION
2 CORINTHIANS 5:11–21

'We are therefore Christ's ambassadors, as though God were making his appeal through us ...' (v.20)

I know there might be some who will say that the main focus of the Church ought to be on overcoming such evils as poverty, famine, violence, unemployment and so on. I most certainly believe that these evils ought to be within the focus of the Christian Church, but they are not to be its main focus. In Britain we have succeeded in abolishing poverty among much of our population. Yet our greatest need remains unmet and many people are on route to a godless eternity. When a well-known preacher conducted a two-week crusade in a certain town, and preached every night from the text, 'You must be born again', someone asked him why he did it. 'It's simple,' he said, 'you must be born again.'

Father, help us see that our main business is not relieving poverty or overcoming social ills, but bringing men and women to Jesus Christ. May Your priority be our priority. Amen.

'They will listen'

FOR READING AND MEDITATION
ACTS 28:17–31

'… this message of the salvation of God has been sent to the Gentiles, and they will listen!' (v.28, Amp)

Paul is speaking to the Jews, and telling them if they will not listen, then the Gentiles will. Every time I stand up to speak in an evangelistic service, I say to myself: 'They will listen.' I said it in Hong Kong when invited to address a rowdy and boisterous group of students. When my turn came to speak, I found that within five minutes, one could have heard a pin drop. This was not due to my ability to captivate an audience, but to the content of the message. I simply told them, 'Your hearts are homesick – homesick for God. You are confused and empty, and can't stand the emptiness.' Believe me, if we aim our words at where men and women are hurting – whoever they are – they will listen.

O Father, I see that since You have planted deep in the heart of man a desire for Yourself, I have an ally in every human soul. Help me to tune in to this wondrous fact and use it to advantage. Amen.

The lay ministry

FOR READING AND MEDITATION
I PETER 2:1–10

'But you are a chosen people, a royal priesthood, a holy nation, a people belonging to God ...' (v.9)

The next mark of a Christian church is *the existence of a strong and vigorous lay ministry*. I wish the term 'lay ministry' had never been coined. It was never God's purpose for His Church to be viewed in terms of ministers and laity, for everyone in the Body of Christ is to be a 'minister'. The way in which I am using the term 'lay ministry' here is in relation to those ministries in the Body of Christ that are performed by those who are unpaid, 'unordained' (in the denominational sense), and have not undergone any formal preparatory training. All of us, paid or unpaid, are involved in contributing to the health, growth and development of the Christian Church.

Father, I am so thankful for the way You are breaking down the barriers between pulpit and pew, and showing us that the ministry in Your Body is one ministry. Amen.

APRIL 11

One Body

FOR READING AND MEDITATION
1 CORINTHIANS 12:1–27

'Now you are the body of Christ, and each one of you is a part of it.' (v.27)

The most prominent metaphor used by Paul to describe the Church is that of a 'body'. This chapter begins with the declaration that all Christians share in the same Spirit (vv.1–3). The Spirit has distributed to God's people a variety of gifts (vv.4–11), and has baptised them into one Body (vv.12–13). Nevertheless, the one Body does not consist of one member but of many (v.14), all of whom are necessary for its proper functioning. Elsewhere, Paul develops the truth that God has appointed five special ministries – apostolic, prophetic, pastoral, evangelism and teaching – all to equip God's people for work in His service (Eph. 4:11–12). Note – *all* people for works of service.

O Father, I see so clearly that when Your Church fails to grasp the truth that it is 'one Body', it fails to function in the way that it was designed. Help us to get things straight. Amen.

Jesus – a layman?

FOR READING AND MEDITATION
LUKE 7:18–23

*'The blind receive sight, the lame walk, those who have
leprosy are cured, the deaf hear, the dead are raised ...'*
(v.22)

The Christian movement began with what we would
describe today as 'laymen'. Jesus was a layman.
He had no credentials that would satisfy the Jewish
leaders, but if they had had eyes to see, they would have
recognised that He was surrounded by all the credentials
He needed – the transformed men and women who had
benefited from His dynamic and miraculous ministry.
The apostles also were laymen. At the Council of Nicea,
a dramatic thing happened when the lay people were
pushed to the edges of the Church and the clergy took
over. Over the centuries, the laity, on the whole, have
been like spectators in the stands while the clergy have
been on the field playing the game. This was never God's
intention.

*Father, I am encouraged to see that, at long last, Your
Church is awakening to the truth that it is one Body and
one ministry and we can all play a part. Amen.*

Clergy coaches

FOR READING AND MEDITATION
EPHESIANS 4:1–16

'From him the whole body ... grows and builds itself up in love, as each part does its work.' (v.16)

In many churches it is the laity who are getting out on the field, while the clergy are standing on the sidelines as coaches. Is this downgrading them? No, upgrading them. It is better to get ten men to do the work than for one man to do the work of ten. Those who are leaders in the Church are failing in their spiritual duty if they do not focus on equipping the lay ministers to function more effectively. Every week the laity should look to the leadership and inwardly say: 'Pastors, we have a task to do that is just too big for us – introduce us to resources that will make us adequate for the task.' That would vitalise listening and vitalise preaching; vitalise the service, vitalise the whole church.

Father, only You can blend the ministries that You have set in Your Body to function in the way You desire. Help us all – clergy and laity – to stand before You with open hearts and open minds. Amen.

'Every member a minister'

FOR READING AND MEDITATION
ROMANS 12:1–8

*'We have different gifts, according to the grace given us
…' (v.6)*

Unfortunately many in today's Church see themselves
not as 'ministers' but as passengers. However, the
future of the Church belongs to the laity – the one people
of God. Some among that one people are given the great
privilege of serving the rest of the Body in the capacity
of an apostle, prophet, pastor, evangelist or teacher. 'The
clergy,' says one well-known London preacher, 'are not
to be viewed as hyphenated to the laity as if they are a
separate class: they are "ministers of the people" because
they themselves belong to the people they are called to
serve.' In our generation we are seeing a rediscovery of
this wonderful truth.

*Father, I am so thankful that I see this turning point in the
life of Your Church. Help me not only to know my place
in Your Body but to function there as You want me to.
Amen.*

Worship first – work second

FOR READING AND MEDITATION
ISAIAH 6:1–13

'Then I heard the voice of the Lord saying, "Whom shall I send?" … And I said, "Here am I. Send me!"' (v.8)

Another mark of a Christian church is *attention to spiritual disciplines.* We read: 'While they were worshipping the Lord and fasting … Then after fasting and praying they put their hands on them and sent them away' (Acts 13:2–3, Amp.). The church at Antioch knew how to worship, pray and fast. The first and foremost duty of a Christian community is not to work for God, but to worship Him. Many churches make the mistake of putting work first and worship second. They take a new convert and make a worker out of him. Our primary aim should not be to make workers out of new converts but worshippers. Worship then leads to work. The worshipper always exclaims 'Here am I. Send me!'

O Father, help me to lay hold on this important truth – that I must first be a worshipper before I become a worker. Teach me to worship You and then work for You. Amen.

The urgent and the important

FOR READING AND MEDITATION
LUKE 10:38–42

'... only one thing is needed. Mary has chosen what is better, and it will not be taken away from her.' (v.42)

We have to be able to discern between what is urgent and what is important. Nowhere is this truth more clearly seen than in today's passage. Martha, busy with her preparations, begins to complain because her sister Mary is sitting and listening to Jesus, rather than helping to get things done. Our Lord, with deep insight, quickly distinguishes between the urgent and the important when He says: 'Mary has chosen what is better.' Have you ever noticed that the Great Commission was given to worshipping people? Matthew records: 'They worshipped ... Then Jesus came to them and said, "... Therefore go and make disciples ... "' (Matt. 28:17–19). Our work for God begins with worship of God.

O God, protect me from the peril of allowing the urgent to crowd out the important. I realise that learning this lesson can transform my entire life – and lifestyle. Amen.

The challenge of fasting

FOR READING AND MEDITATION
MATTHEW 4:1–11

'Then Jesus was led by the Spirit into the desert to be tempted by the devil.' (v.1)

A spiritual fast is simply abstaining from food for a spiritual purpose. Scripture shows that fasting was done for a number of reasons – to seek God's will (Acts 14:23), in repentance for sin (Jonah 3:5), out of concern for God's work (Neh. 1:4), to humble oneself (Psa. 69:10), for greater effectiveness in casting out evil spirits (Mark 9:29) and, as with the community at Antioch, as part of their worship. One of the most important things to learn about fasting is not to approach it legalistically, but to be guided by the Holy Spirit. As today's passage shows, Jesus was led by the Spirit into His forty-day fast. Don't forget that – otherwise you will be brought into bondage.

Father, the deeper I want to go with You, the more challenging the Christian life becomes. But I would not pull back. Help me as I face this immensely challenging issue of fasting. Amen.

Is this God's voice I hear?

FOR READING AND MEDITATION
HEBREWS 3:1–15

'Today, if you hear his voice, do not harden your hearts ...' (v.15)

In Scripture, the normal means of fasting involved abstaining from all food, solid or liquid, but not from water. This is known as a partial fast. There are some examples in Scripture of people abstaining from both food and water (Esth. 4:16; Acts 9:9), and this we call an absolute fast. Although fasting is usually an individual matter, there are occasions in Scripture when people entered into a corporate fast (Joel 2:15; 2 Chron. 20:3). Are Christians merely invited or expected to fast? The Bible is quite clear – we are not only invited to fast but expected to fast. In Matthew 6:16, Jesus said: 'When you fast ...' Be careful, however, if you have serious physical problems, such as diabetes.

O Father, if You are speaking to me directly about the need to fast, then help me not to rationalise the issue but to respond to it. 'Speak, Lord, Your servant is listening.' Amen.

Prayer is education

FOR READING AND MEDITATION
EPHESIANS 6:10–20

'Pray at all times in the Spirit, with all prayer and supplication ...' (v.18, RSV)

S omeone showed me that prayer is an education; it is something we learn. They said: 'You must not expect to jump up through the education system right away: you must graduate – from one level to another.' This helped me greatly and released me from a good deal of tension. If prayer was an education, then I was free to experiment, free to ask questions and free, at times, to fail. Prayer is a spiritual discipline, but it is more than that – it is a joyous discovery. Individually and corporately we need to rediscover the value and power of prayer, for both individual and corporate life, like a watch, have a tendency to run down. Prayer brings resources – the resources of God. Antioch discovered that – so must we.

Father, I have learned much about prayer, but there is so much more I need to learn. So I come again and say, 'Teach me to pray.' Help me, dear Father. Amen.

Who is the Holy Spirit?

FOR READING AND MEDITATION
JOHN 14:15–27

'And I will ask the Father, and he will give you another Counsellor to be with you for ever.' (v.16)

The next mark of the church at Antioch was this – *the voice of the Holy Spirit was heard, giving clear direction and guidance.* The doctrine of the Trinity – ie, one God in three Persons – is not a doctrine of reason, but of revelation. That is to say, we do not believe it because we can reason it out, but we believe it because it is clearly laid down in Scripture. The Holy Spirit is a Person who is as real and as important as the Lord Jesus Christ Himself. It is a question not of one God with three names but one God who is three separate Persons, co-equal, co-eternal and co-existent. If you find it difficult to understand, don't let that discourage you, for a God who is fully understood by mortals is no God.

Father, as I struggle to grasp this tremendous truth that You are 'three in one and one in three', give me Your divine illumination and understanding. Amen.

God – the Holy Spirit

FOR READING AND MEDITATION
2 CORINTHIANS 13:1–14

'May the grace of the Lord Jesus Christ, and the love of God, and the fellowship of the Holy Spirit be with you all.' (v.14)

The disciples were Jews who believed in just one God. Gradually they came to realise that Jesus was God in human form (eg, Matt. 16:16; John 20:28). Following Christ's ascension into heaven, the Holy Spirit came to indwell the Christian believers, and after a while the conviction began to dawn upon them that the Holy Spirit was not just a power, but a Person. From the earliest days of the Church, the conviction grew that God, Christ and the Holy Spirit were one in three and three in one – a conviction that came to be summarised in the inspired declaration before us today. I say again, we are here at the central mystery of our most holy faith. Let us bow and adore the great Triune God.

Father, Son and Holy Spirit, I bow before the wonder of Your greatness and Your might. Deepen my comprehension of Your nature, and help me see that I can stand even when I cannot understand. Amen.

The Spirit's specific function

FOR READING AND MEDITATION
ACTS 21:1–14

'The Holy Spirit says, "In this way the Jews of Jerusalem will bind the owner of this belt and will hand him over to the Gentiles."' (v.11)

The Holy Spirit, just like the other two Persons of the Trinity, contributes to the growth of the Church in specific ways. One of the ways in which the Holy Spirit guides His Church is by speaking to them. Some point to the incident in Acts where the Spirit subjectively conveyed to the group who had gathered an inner impression concerning God's will: 'It seemed good to the Holy Spirit and to us' (Acts 15:28). Others refer to Acts 13:2–3: 'The Holy Spirit said, "Separate for me Barnabas and Saul for the work to which I have called them."' We conclude that both are valid ways in which the Spirit guides: sometimes subjectively through an inner impression; at other times, objectively through the spoken word.

O Father, forgive us for the times we push ahead with our self-centred plans, instead of pausing to heed what the Spirit wants to say to us. Teach us how to recognise and be led by Your voice. Amen.

'The heart throb of the Spirit'

FOR READING AND MEDITATION
I THESSALONIANS 5:12–24

'Do not quench the Spirit.' (v.19, NASB)

S ome churches overemphasise the Holy Spirit and they become extreme. Others, desirous of being open to the Holy Spirit but yet not wanting to be dubbed as 'charismatic', avoid the issue altogether. The church at Antioch, like the rest of the New Testament churches, was a church in which the Holy Spirit was both expected and given the freedom to speak. Many of today's churches lack 'the heart throb of the Spirit' as we do not expect Him to speak because we reason that after 2,000 years of experience we are no longer in need of supernatural intervention. However, a church that fails to seek or expect the mind of God to be made known in its midst is a church that is run by men and not by God.

O God, help us to see that if Your Spirit is not at work in our midst, then we are nothing more than lighthouses in which there is no light. In Jesus' name we pray. Amen.

'When we listen – God speaks'

FOR READING AND MEDITATION
REVELATION 3:7–13

'He who has an ear, let him hear what the Spirit says to the churches.' (v.13)

The Antioch church was spiritually sensitised to supernatural intervention: 'while they were worshipping the Lord and fasting' the Spirit spoke. Worship and fasting, like prayer and fasting, sensitises the soul so that it learns to listen. Perhaps that's another reason why we don't hear God's voice speaking to us today as much as they did in New Testament times – we have not learned how to listen. For, as Blaise Pascal used to say, 'When we listen – God speaks.' Worship in the Early Church was not just pouring out praise and adoration to God, but being alert to who He was and what He wanted to do. Worship, you see, is not just offering God words, but offering Him our obedient selves to do what He says.

O Father, forgive us for not listening. Teach us how to prepare ourselves so that Your voice will not go unnoticed or unheeded in our midst. For Your own dear name's sake we ask it. Amen.

The world for God

FOR READING AND MEDITATION
MARK 16:14–20

'Go into all the world and preach the good news to all creation.' (v.15)

The final mark of a Christian church is *a worldwide vision*. The church at Antioch won people to Christ around their home base, but prompted by the Spirit, they were participants in sending out the gospel to the whole world. Barnabas and Saul, backed by the church and under the direction of the Holy Spirit, started one of the greatest missionary outreaches that ever touched our planet. One observer said, 'The Christian faith has … no rivals in the work of human redemption. There isn't a spot on earth where they have been allowed to go where they haven't brought the things that lift the soul – churches, schools, hospitals, leper colonies and homes for the blind. No other movement has done anything like it.'

O Father, I see yet again what can happen when a church stops and listens, for nothing can truly happen in the world until Your Church listens. Help us hear You clearly. Amen.

The call must be confirmed

FOR READING AND MEDITATION
2 CORINTHIANS 8:10–24

'What is more, he was chosen by the churches to accompany us …' (v.19)

When God chose Mary as the vessel through whom His Son should be born into the world, He broke the news to her personally. So God's call to special service can come directly through a personal revelation. It can come through divinely arranged circumstances when 'things just work out right'. The call to special service can come also, as it did in Antioch, through prophetic intimation. We do not quite know how the voice of God broke through to the group who were gathered, but it seems reasonable to assume that it would have come through one of the prophets. No matter how the call comes, one thing is sure – at some point it must always be confirmed by the people of God.

Father, I am so thankful for the trust and confidence You place in Your Church. Help us to be worthy of that trust, especially in our recognition of those who are called to special service. Amen.

'Go forward within the fellowship'

FOR READING AND MEDITATION
ACTS 15:1–22

'The church sent them on their way ...' (v.3)

There are many who feel they have a calling from God, but fail to recognise that at some point that calling must be confirmed by the church. God has protected His Church from charlatans, and even those who are just misguided, by giving every local church the authority, through its leadership, either to confirm or reject a so-called 'ministry'. Campbell Morgan, the great Bible expositor, put it this way: 'If a man hears the call of God, then let him remember it is his business to go forward within the fellowship and under the guidance of the church.' It must have meant a lot to Barnabas and Saul to know that they were being sent out, not only by the Holy Spirit, but also by the church.

O Father, I am so grateful for the security I feel in being part, not only of You, but of Your Church. In the visible, I meet the Invisible; through the tangible, the Intangible. I am so grateful. Amen.

The evil of parochialism

FOR READING AND MEDITATION
ISAIAH 50:1–11

'... is my hand shortened, that it cannot redeem? Or have I no power to deliver?' (v.2, RSV)

How does the attitude of the Church of today compare with that of the Christian community at Antioch? Not very well, I am sorry to say. Far too many of today's churches have restricted vision, and see no further than the frontiers of their own vicinity or parish. Any Christian community that settles for less than the world as its parish is acting as though the Lord's arm has somehow lost its power to save. No one local church can save the world, but does it long to save the world? Does its concern spill over beyond its parochial boundaries and consider also the world's needs? One great spiritual leader said: 'The world is my parish, and all who perish are in that parish.'

O God, deliver us, we pray, from the evil of parochialism. Help us to see that 'the world is our parish and all who perish are in that parish'. For Your own dear name's sake. Amen.

Clarifying our vision

FOR READING AND MEDITATION
PROVERBS 29:1–18

'Where there is no vision, the people perish ...' (v.18, AV)

It has always intrigued me that a church which develops a spiritual concern for the needs of the world is almost invariably a church where great things happen. How interested are we in what is going on in the countries of the Third World? How much do we pray for them? How much do we give to them? How real and 'alive' is our concern? If we cannot send missionaries to other lands for long periods of service, then we can do the next best thing and send short-term missionaries to encourage the local believers to forge ahead with the work of preaching the gospel. The Holy Spirit, who is God's agent for creation (Gen. 1:2), inspires into creativity all those who are in touch with Him.

O Father, help us to offer You all our powers so that they may be touched into creativity. Create, I pray, hope, vision, courage, inspiration and spiritual daring in the midst of Your Church. Amen.

'Marching orders'

FOR READING AND MEDITATION
JOHN 8:12–32

'Again Jesus spoke to them, saying, "I am the light of the world …"' (v.12, RSV)

Suppose a whole church laid themselves open to God in worship, fasting and spiritual expectancy – what would happen? Would they hear just words of comfort and communion? Perhaps so, but I think they would hear something else – they would be given their 'marching orders'. As long as the Lord delays His coming, there will always be work for His servants to do. We must meet the obligation, not because we are shining examples of the faith or because we are personally superior to others, but because He is the Light of the World. We must claim the whole world in His name. The acts of the church at Antioch pulsated with such vitality that the disciples were first called 'Christians' there.

Gracious Father, I pray that You will make us into the image of the group at Antioch. And may the Holy Spirit, in turn, make us into Christ's image so that we may be called Christians. Amen.

There's more!

FOR READING AND MEDITATION
ACTS 1:1–11

'You will receive power when the Holy Spirit comes on you ...' (v.8)

If we draw a line through the pages of the New Testament we will find on one side a good deal of spiritual fumbling and inadequacy. It is all very sub-Christian. On the other side, however, we find spiritual poise, power and certainty. It is all very Christian. That line runs straight through an upper room where a group of people waited in prayer for the promise their Master made to them. After Pentecost these timid and hesitant disciples got hold of something that set them ablaze and made them into men who were invincible. Whereas before they appeared to be working with cold chisels, now they were working with – dynamite. However much of the Spirit you have received, believe me – there's more!

Father, I sense I am on the verge of being introduced to more of what I know I need and what I long for – divine power and divine purity. Take over within. In Jesus' name. Amen.

Teacher and doer

FOR READING AND MEDITATION
JOHN 1:19–34

'… he … will baptise with the Holy Spirit.' (v.33)

Although the actual experience of receiving the Holy Spirit was new to these disciples, our Lord had exposed them to a course of training in preparation for this event. We find this course unfolded best in John's Gospel. There are twelve lessons and the first is where John discloses the truth that 'the man on whom you see the Spirit come down and remain is he who will baptise with the Holy Spirit'. This Man possessed the Spirit in human surroundings and conditions, demonstrated its meaning there, and gives the Spirit to others in the same surroundings and conditions. In other words, Christ not only teaches us the truth about the Holy Spirit but has demonstrated those truths also. A teacher and doer.

Lord Jesus, I am so glad that what You teach me are not just ideas but issues that You have experienced Yourself. You have worn my flesh, measured my humanity and know just what I need. Amen.

Come, Holy Spirit, come

FOR READING AND MEDITATION
ACTS 10:23-48

'While Peter was still speaking … the Holy Spirit came on all who heard the message.' (v.44)

I once attended a church where the preacher announced his text from Acts 1:8, but the only reference to the Holy Spirit came at the end of the sermon: 'Come, Holy Spirit, come and dwell with us.' That was all. You can imagine my disappointment as I left that church feeling I had been given a title rather than teaching, a label rather than life. The sermon was quite brilliant, but it was the brilliance of moonlight. What the congregation needed was not moonlight but sunlight. What is the good of admitting the existence of the Holy Spirit if we have no experience of Him? Is not this why the faith of many modern-day Christians is weak and anaemic? They lack the red blood of the Spirit's life within their veins.

Father, help me not to be one who believes in the existence of the Holy Spirit but has no experience of Him. If Jesus needed to be empowered by the Spirit then how much more do I? Amen.

Needed – an earthquake

FOR READING AND MEDITATION
ACTS 4:23–37

'… they were all filled with the Holy Spirit and spoke the word of God boldly.' (v.31)

Recently, I read of a parish in which the bishop announced to all the clergy that he was proposing they make Pentecost Sunday a special Quiet Day. One vicar wrote to the bishop and said: 'What our parish needs is not a Quiet Day but an earthquake.' Augustine described those who were part of the Christian community but not really converted as 'frost-bound followers'. They needed the warm glow of the Spirit's converting power to unfreeze them. Sam Shoemaker, an Episcopalian minister in the United States who helped start Alcoholics Anonymous, used to say: 'Some people have enough of religion to make them feel uneasy in a gambling joint, but not enough to make them feel at home in a prayer meeting.'

O God, it is clear some parts of Your Church need not a Quiet Day but an Earthshaking Day. Break in upon us by Your power and shake us out of our sickening ease and complacency. Amen.

The fire-baptising Christ

FOR READING AND MEDITATION
MATTHEW 3:1–12

'He will baptise you with the Holy Spirit and with fire.'
(v.11)

We look now at two vital notes that John strikes about the One on whom the Spirit would rest: 'Look, the Lamb of God, who takes away the sin of the world!' (John 1:29), and 'He ... will baptise with the Holy Spirit' (John 1:33). John specialised in the baptism of water – immersing people into the cold, murky waters of the Jordan. But Jesus would specialise in the baptism of the Spirit – immersing people not into cold water but into fire! Our Lord never baptised with water. He would usher in the era of the Spirit, when God would work not from the outside in, but from the inside out. Should not our greatest concern be how we can make His baptism ours?

Blessed Holy Spirit, however much of the heavenly fire is at work in me, fan it into a mightier blaze, I pray. Come, Holy Spirit, come, and light on the altar of my heart Your eternal flame. Amen.

No need for fear

FOR READING AND MEDITATION
LUKE 11:1-13

'Which of you fathers, if your son asks for a fish, will give him a snake instead?' (v.11)

The fact that the Spirit is given through Jesus means we need never be afraid to open ourselves to divine power. Jesus was passionate but never ever unbalanced. Jesus is the revelation of God's nature and also God's power. He got His guidance in the same way we get our guidance – through prayer and meditation on the Scriptures. We ought not to be afraid of being made like Him, but rather of not being like Him. If we are filled by the Holy Spirit we will be made like Him. The Holy Spirit is of the same character and nature as Jesus. That is why the Holy Spirit will never lead you to do anything that is unlike Jesus. There is no need to fear the Holy Spirit for His power is power after the character of Jesus.

Father, thank You for making clear that the nature of the Spirit is the nature of Jesus. Now I need not be afraid of surrendering to Him, for I am not afraid of surrendering to Jesus. Amen.

Twice born

FOR READING AND MEDITATION
JOHN 3:1–21

'… unless a man is born of water and the Spirit, he cannot enter the kingdom of God.' (v.5)

The second lesson is that no one can be either filled or empowered by the Spirit until he or she is born into the kingdom of God by the Spirit. And how is a person born into the kingdom? By two things: by *water*, and by *the Spirit*. Some think that 'being born of water' has to do with one's physical birth, and 'being born of the Spirit' has to do with the regeneration of one's inner being. However, most Christian commentators reject this view and believe that the term 'water' has to do with John's baptism of repentance, and has within it also a prophetic element relating to what would come later – Christian baptism. The point is that it is possible to be outwardly born of water but not born of the Spirit.

Father, help me understand that without the birth of the Spirit I cannot have the blessings of the Spirit. I must pass from the once born to the twice born. Amen.

'You need God'

FOR READING AND MEDITATION
2 CORINTHIANS 5:11–21

'… if anyone is in Christ, he is a new creation …' (v.17)

Acouple who were on the verge of bankruptcy decided to sell their furniture, listen to some beautiful music, go on a drunken binge and then separate. When they told their story to a Christian furniture dealer he said: 'Look here, what you need more than listening to beautiful music is God.' They admitted it, knelt with him in prayer and found God. If they had tried only to impose beautiful music on the inner disharmonies of their lives and had never surrendered to God they would have ended up in despair. When we work from the outside in, we experience frustration. When we allow God through the Holy Spirit to work from the inside out, we finish up in fellowship with Him, with ourselves and with others.

Father, I am grateful that You do not try to change me by tinkering around on the outside. You go straight to the heart of the issue – within. Thank You that You are 'within'. Amen.

'No grandchildren'

FOR READING AND MEDITATION
1 JOHN 3:1–24

'Everyone who has this hope in him purifies himself, just as he is pure.' (v.3)

We come into the kingdom of God through the birth of the Spirit, or not at all. As someone put it: 'God has no grandchildren.' But how do we define this birth of the Spirit? Is it something sudden or is it something gradual? It can be either. I love the definition of the new birth given first, I think, by Dr E.S. Jones, who said: 'The birth of the Spirit is that change, gradual or sudden, by which we who are the children of the first birth, through a physical birth into a physical world, become children of the second birth, through a spiritual birth into a spiritual world.' A Christian is someone who has been born twice. You must have a spiritual birth to enter the kingdom of God.

Father, while I am deeply thankful for my first birth, I am eternally thankful for my second birth. And I am grateful that above all I can call You Abba, Father! Amen.

Dead or alive?

FOR READING AND MEDITATION
EPHESIANS 2:1–18

*'Because of his great love for us, God ... made us alive
with Christ ...' (v.5)*

These verses make it clear that the birth of the Spirit is quite different from our natural birth. *'Children born not of natural descent'* (John 1:13). Our parents can give us much but they can't give us salvation. A Christian home may give us a push in the direction of Christ, but it can't bring us eternal life. We are children of God, 'not by natural descent, *nor of human decision'*. It is not a matter of whipping up the will, striving a little harder, being a little more faithful in religious exercises, or being more regular in church attendance. No one finds God by climbing the ladder of self-effort, rung by rung, to find Him on the topmost rung, having got there by human worthiness and merit.

O God, I want to thank You that I am not just alive, but alive for evermore. Amen.

A limitless coming

FOR READING AND MEDITATION
JOHN 3:22–36

'… the one whom God has sent … to him God gives the
Spirit without limit.' (v.34)

We look now at the third lesson in the 'School of
the Spirit' as unfolded in John's Gospel. If Christ
is to be given the Spirit 'without limit' then it suggests
that prior to this the Holy Spirit was given in a limited,
temporary way. The limitation, I hasten to add, was not
in the Spirit Himself but in the Spirit's difficulty in finding
men and women to whom He could give Himself without
measure. The Old Testament believers looked forward to a
day when the Spirit would be given not merely on special
occasions and for special purposes but would come to
preside and reside in the midst of humanity for ever. Are
you aware that you and I are living in that day?

O Father, I see clearly that however wonderful was the
ministry of the Holy Spirit in Old Testament times, His
ministry in the New is even more wonderful. Thank You
that I am part of His purposes. Amen.

When the 'best' fall

FOR READING AND MEDITATION
PSALM 51:1–19

'Against you, you only, have I sinned and done what is evil in your sight …' (v.4)

K ing David was said to be a man 'after God's own heart' yet he coveted Bathsheba for himself, seduced her and then planned the death of her husband. This psalm is, in fact, the record of his confession. Why did God use such people whose lives lacked holiness? The answer is this – God used these imperfect people as a point in a line, taking care all the time to teach and show that there would come One who would be the perfect vehicle for His purposes. Through Him the main work of the Spirit – holiness – would be advanced ad infinitum in the world. And who was that perfect vehicle? I think you know. Jesus!

O Father, the more I learn, the more grateful I am that One has come into the world who shows me not only how to live but who, through the Spirit, empowers me to avoid sin. Amen.

God's greatest pleasure

FOR READING AND MEDITATION
JOEL 2:21–32

'… I will pour out my Spirit on all people.' (v.28)

The verse before us today is probably one of the most outstanding declarations of the Old Testament concerning the Holy Spirit. It promises that the day will come when the Spirit will no longer be given occasionally and temporarily, but constantly and perpetually. Although God uses the imperfect to advance His purposes, He does not take pleasure in unrighteousness. He takes *pleasure* in holiness. Many years ago, I spoke to a group of converted drug addicts in a basement in Soho, London, on the work and ministry of the Holy Spirit. One of them blurted out in the middle of my address: 'I've got it: the Spirit is given to make me as pure and holy as Jesus is.' He is.

Holy Spirit – Your very name suggests that one of Your prime concerns is to maintain holiness in the world. Make me a holy person and then I shall be a whole person. In Jesus' name. Amen.

'Life Ltd'

FOR READING AND MEDITATION
JOHN 10:1–21

'… I have come that they may have life, and have it to the full.' (v.10)

The Spirit was active in the lives of the disciples prior to their experience of Him in the Upper Room. But however He worked and whatever He accomplished, it was quite different from what He did in them and for them at Pentecost. Before they had life, but now they had it more abundantly. Before they had joy, but now they had joy with a bubble in it. Before they had peace, but now it was peace like a river. It seems that prior to Pentecost whatever they had of the Spirit was limited; after Pentecost it appeared to be *limitless*. What they had *overflowed*. A sign could be put up over many Christian lives: 'Life Ltd'. And yet Jesus said the purpose of His coming is to give life 'more abundantly'.

O God, forgive me that I am content to enjoy life rather than life to the full. I open my whole being to You today and ask that Your Spirit will come in and fill me to overflowing. Amen.

The door is open

FOR READING AND MEDITATION
PSALM 65:1–13

'You crown the year with your bounty, and your carts overflow with abundance.' (v.11)

If you believe that you had the fullness of the Spirit at conversion then my question is: Are you allowing the Spirit to flow through you in the way so clearly depicted in the New Testament? Are you living life *abundantly*? And to those who claim to have received a second experience of the Spirit subsequent to their conversion I would put this question: Have you quenched the work of the Spirit in your heart, or are you as much on fire for God now as then? Our beliefs are important, but belief must be seen to have an effect on our behaviour. Are we experiencing trickles of the Holy Spirit or a mighty Niagara? The Spirit is given to bring us from life limited to life unlimited. The door is open; go on through.

Father, forgive me for thinking that what I have been reading these past few days does not apply to me. Your promise is to me. Me! Help me go through any door You may be opening for me. Amen.

'Me!'

FOR READING AND MEDITATION
JOHN 7:25–44

'On the last ... day of the Feast, Jesus ... said ... "If a man is thirsty, let him come to me and drink."' (v.37)

The next lesson is: *the Spirit would not be given in fullness until Jesus was glorified.* On the last day of the Feast of Tabernacles the priest took an empty pitcher down to the Pool of Siloam, filled it with water, brought it up to the Temple courtyard and poured the water into the dust. Jesus saw the people entering into the pageantry and ceremony of the Feast of Tabernacles, but with no true realisation of where life was to be found. Today some people are more taken up with the rituals of the Church than with the Lord of the Church. The thirst that is in our souls can never be quenched by religious ceremonies; it can only be quenched through a personal encounter with Christ.

Lord Jesus, forgive me if I have sought to quench the thirst of my soul in something other than You. Whatever I enjoy about my religion, help me see that only in You can my soul be satisfied. Amen.

The inexhaustible life

FOR READING AND MEDITATION
JOHN 4:1–24

'… but whoever drinks the water I give him will never thirst.' (v.14)

Those who drink of Christ and the Spirit find they are linked to infinite resources. And the more we draw on those resources the more we have. There is no danger of exhausting those resources, for however much we draw upon them, there is always more. Christians must stop thinking of themselves as a reservoir with only limited resources, and that, if they draw upon them, they have only so much left. This idea will result in us measuring what we give rather than giving extravagantly. We must get hold of the fact that we are channels linked to infinite resources – resources that simply can never run dry. This is not just the abundant life, this is the inexhaustible life.

O Father, how thrilled I am to know that Your supplies exceed my greatest demands. Forgive me that I scrape the bottom of the barrel when there are at Your disposal riches immeasurable. Amen.

'A face lift?'

FOR READING AND MEDITATION
ROMANS 8:1–17

'[He] will also give life to your mortal bodies through his Spirit …' (v.11)

In John 7:38 the Greek for 'within him' refers to the heart or the inner being. The effects of the coming of the Holy Spirit will rejuvenate us not only spiritually but physically too. A man said that prior to his conversion and the filling of the Spirit he used to wear his shoes out at the heel. After the Spirit had come to dwell in him he discovered that he wore his shoes out at the toes. He carefully considered why this should be, and he concluded that the coming of the Spirit had tipped his whole life forward – physically as well as spiritually. One lady I heard of was asked by a friend: 'You look so well; have you had a facelift?' 'No, my dear,' was her reply. 'But I have met Jesus!'

O Spirit of God, when You are allowed to work within me You will not stop until You work on all of me – spirit, soul and body. Quicken my brain cells and give me a better functioning body. Amen.

Demanding or donating?

FOR READING AND MEDITATION
ACTS 20:13-38

'... the Lord Jesus himself said: "It is more blessed to give than to receive."' (v.35)

We are designed to focus on giving to others not getting from others. The 'streams of living water' that are said to flow out of us are: 'love, joy, peace, patience, kindness, goodness, faithfulness, gentleness and self-control' (Gal. 5:22–23). Note they begin with 'love' and end with 'self-control'. This is because the Christian method of self-control is not to sit on yourself in a strong determined effort to keep yourself under control, but to express yourself under the law of love – you love God supremely and then every other lesser love falls into place naturally and normally. You become not just a full person but also a fulfilled person.

O God, I see that I must be a donating and not a demanding person. Satiate my being with Your Holy Spirit so that I will not seek to draw from others, but give to them. Amen.

Our Saviour's glorification

FOR READING AND MEDITATION
I PETER 2:13–25

'He himself bore our sins in his body on the tree ...' (v.24)

Why couldn't the Spirit be given until Jesus was glorified? Apparently for two reasons. First, it was necessary for Christ to be glorified as Saviour on the cross and then glorified as Sovereign on the throne. Take the first – *glorified as Saviour on the cross*. Sin had created such a chasm between humanity and God that before the resources of the Spirit could be fully given to us, a way had to be found for that chasm to be bridged and sin to be forgiven. God certainly forgave sin in Old Testament times, but He could not flow into people's lives with all the cleansing energy and power of the Spirit. To put it another way – Calvary had to become a finality before Pentecost could become a reality.

Lord Jesus, Your glory is my glory. For in being glorified as Sovereign and Saviour You have ensured my glorification in eternity. I am eternally grateful. Amen.

King of glory!

FOR READING AND MEDITATION
PSALM 24:1–10

'Lift up your heads, O you gates … that the King of glory may come in.' (v.7)

When Christ came to this earth He temporarily gave up His place on the throne, and while never ceasing to be what He had always been – true God – He became what He had never been before – true man. Following His ascension, however, He returned to the throne and took up the role of Sovereign once again. God was well pleased with His Son and crowned Him with a crown that He had never had before – King of humanity. And if there had been any doubt in the minds of those who had seen Him ascend to heaven as to whether or not His mission was completed, all such doubts would have been removed on the Day of Pentecost. It was as if our Lord sent back a telegram saying, 'Arrived safely. All is well!'

Father, I rejoice that because all is well in heaven, all is well with me. My security depends on what happens on that throne and I know that what happens there will be for my good. Amen.

For ever!

FOR READING AND MEDITATION
JOHN 14:1–17

'… the Father … will give you another Counsellor to be with you for ever …' (v.16)

Today's verse brings out the fifth lesson about the Spirit from John's Gospel: that the Spirit's coming would not be a temporary coming; He would abide with them for ever. An occasional coming is replaced by a permanent indwelling. The Holy Spirit would not come and go – a kind of furtive, sporadic, hide-and-seek approach; He would move within the inner recesses of our being and be there for ever. The only way He would leave would be by conscious, deliberate, continuous, and purposeful sin. An occasional lapse into sin would not break that relationship. It might cloud it and mar it, but He would still be there, ready to restore and re-establish the interrupted intimacy. For, after all, He is the Spirit not only of power but also of grace.

Tender and loving Holy Spirit, I am grateful that though You draw back in the presence of sin, You plead with me until I break with sin, and remain with me for ever. Amen.

'The Holy Guest'

FOR READING AND MEDITATION
I JOHN 2:15–29

'As for you, the anointing you received from him remains in you …' (v.27)

Some Christians view the Holy Spirit only through the pages of the Old Testament, forgetting that there the revelation concerning the Spirit is progressive; in the New Testament it is final. A theologian said: 'The Holy Spirit is forever, or He is futile.' The Holy Ghost is referred to by some Christians as the Holy Guest. I have no objection to this except to add that He is a permanent Guest. He does not come and go. He stays – permanently. I say again, there is almost nothing so important as getting hold of this, for if we think the possession of the Spirit is only tentative and momentary then this defeats the very purpose of redemption.

Gracious Spirit, I now see something that I have always wanted to see and for which my heart craves – You taking up Your permanent abode in my being. Amen.

Fullness into power

FOR READING AND MEDITATION
LUKE 4:1–14

'When the devil had finished all this tempting, he left him until an opportune time.' (v.13)

Jesus returned from the Jordan 'full of the Holy Spirit' and was then 'led by the Spirit in the desert, where for forty days he was tempted by the devil'. Fancy being 'led by the Spirit' into a desert. Wouldn't you suppose the Spirit would lead our Lord away from the desert or even around the desert? But no, because in the midst of the desert He was in the perfect centre of God's will. I just love the verse in this passage that tells us that after the forty-day temptation was over, 'Jesus returned to Galilee in the power of the Spirit ...' (v.14). Because the Spirit was within Him, all that temptation could do was to turn fullness into power. In our desert times the Spirit is still with us whether we feel Him or not.

Father, I see that the secret of life is to have the Spirit within. Fortified by Him I am ready to face the most barren desert. When I supply the willingness You always supply the power. Amen.

The Divine Counsellor

FOR READING AND MEDITATION
JOHN 8:31–41

'Then you will know the truth, and the truth will set you free.' (v.32)

The translators of the NIV called the Holy Spirit a Counsellor in John 14:16 rather than a Comforter or Helper, because of the force of the original Greek word *para* which means 'beside', and *kaleo* which means 'call'. The Holy Spirit is therefore One who is called alongside to counsel, encourage and support. Then note also that the Divine Counsellor, the Holy Spirit, is called the 'Spirit of truth'. He not only brings truth to us, but He Himself is the essence of truth, the Spirit of truth. He counsels us by exposing the lies we cling to and revealing the truth to us. He frees us by getting us to identify with truth, and then as we take the truth on board – the truth sets us free.

O Spirit of God and Spirit of truth, counsel me according to Your Word – the Word of truth. You love me too much to let me get away with anything that will harm me. Amen.

'Exactly like'

FOR READING AND MEDITATION
LUKE 12:1–12

'… for the Holy Spirit will teach you at that time what you should say.' (v.12)

Note the phrase 'another Counsellor' (John 14:16). Without that 'another' the word 'Counsellor' is undefined. Our Lord is really saying here that the Holy Spirit would exercise a ministry of counselling like His own. In the Greek, the word for 'another' means 'exactly like'. The love this new Counsellor would show, the power He would exert, the character He would display, the insights He would give, the wisdom He would impart, would be 'exactly like' that of Jesus. This is why we ought never to be afraid of the Holy Spirit, for He is Christlike in everything He says and does. We can ask for nothing higher; we can be content with nothing less.

Holy Spirit, I am so glad that You are a Counsellor equal to Jesus. All that He was You are. Thus I have at my disposal the greatest counselling team in the universe. I am so thankful. Amen.

Teacher and 'Remembrancer'

FOR READING AND MEDITATION
JOHN 14:15–31

'The Counsellor … will teach you all things and will remind you of everything I have said to you.' (v.26)

The sixth lesson that John's Gospel unfolds concerning the ministry of the Holy Spirit is this – He will be a Teacher and a 'Remembrancer'. I am not suggesting that the Holy Spirit is going to write a new Bible for us, but He will open up the Bible we have in a way that at times will be quite astonishing. Christianity is a religion of absolutes, such as the absolute that there is only one God and salvation is only through faith in Christ. But within those absolutes there is provision for a growing understanding and a growing revelation. I believe with all my heart there are insights and concepts in the Bible yet to be discovered. And how do we discover them? By letting the Holy Spirit teach us.

Father, I see that Your Word is both fixed and unfolding. The one end of my compass needle is fixed in You and in Your Word while the other sweeps the horizons with the Holy Spirit. Amen.

Knowing the Author

FOR READING AND MEDITATION
1 CORINTHIANS 2:1–16

'… the things that come from the Spirit of God … are
spiritually discerned.' (v.14)

For a person to understand the Bible by the human
intellect alone is just as impossible as it is for a blind
man to judge a beauty contest. It is possible to undergo
a four-year course in theology, obtain a degree in the
subject, know the Bible from beginning to end, answer
any question on it, memorise large parts of it, and still not
understand it. The natural mind (ie the mind without the
Spirit) does not understand the intentions and purposes
of God. To know and understand an author one must
usually read his book, but to understand the Bible – that
is *really* understand it – one must first know the Author.
When you know the Author, then He, through the Holy
Spirit, teaches it to you.

*O Father, how can I thank You enough for revealing Yourself
to me? Now, because I know You, I can know Your Word,
the Bible. Teach it to me, Father, in and through Your Holy
Spirit. Amen.*

The heavenly Eliezer

FOR READING AND MEDITATION
GENESIS 24:1–66

'"Who is that man in the field coming to meet us?" "He is my master," the servant answered.' (v.65)

I think the first thing the Holy Spirit teaches must be the greatness and uniqueness of our Lord Jesus Christ. How beautifully today's passage illustrates what God is doing at present in the world. On the long journey home I can imagine Eliezer speaking constantly of Isaac and his qualities. Now God has sent the Holy Spirit, the heavenly Eliezer, to seek a bride for His Son. Because you and I have been found by Him, He is travelling with us through life, teaching us everything we need to know about Jesus and highlighting His every quality and characteristic. Believe me, nothing delights the Holy Spirit more than to turn the spotlight on Jesus and create in our hearts a longing to see His face.

Blessed Lord Jesus, now I see why there is such a longing in me to meet with You in eternity and see Your face. The Holy Spirit is doing His work well. I am so grateful. Amen.

The historic Jesus

FOR READING AND MEDITATION
1 JOHN 4:1–21

'Every spirit that acknowledges that Jesus Christ has come in the flesh is from God ...' (v.2)

The Holy Spirit delights to teach us the historicity of Christ. I mean by this the fact that God in Jesus actually came to this earth in bodily form. Some early religious groups denied this and lost their focus. When we are not under the Spirit's guidance we become fixed on some things that Jesus taught but neglect the 'everything'. We alight on one thing and that one thing becomes everything. The consequence is a lop-sided Christianity with an overemphasis on some things and a neglect of other things. This is why we have so many different denominations. One group says this is the most important truth and lifts it high above the others; another group, something else. It is possible to live on a truth instead of on the Truth.

O Spirit of God, take from my heart all desire to focus on just one truth to the exclusion of others. I don't want to live on a truth, I want to live on all the truth. Help me, Holy Spirit. Amen.

The 'Strengthener'

FOR READING AND MEDITATION
2 CORINTHIANS 3:7–18

'We ... are being transformed into his likeness with ever-increasing glory ...' (v.18)

Some translations use the word 'Strengthener' instead of 'Counsellor', and although it is not the best translation it is nevertheless quite a good one. I can remember my pastor telling me when I was a teenager: 'The Holy Spirit will make you Christlike.' I felt rather threatened by that statement because I saw Christlikeness in terms of seriousness and solemnity. I was a fun-loving teenager and I didn't want anything that would curb my personality. However, I came to see that Christlikeness, far from curbing the personality, completes it. Now I have learned not to be afraid of Christlikeness. I just let myself go and allow the Holy Spirit's strength to make me more and more like Him.

O God my Father, I am not afraid of being like Jesus; I am more afraid of being unlike Him. May the Holy Spirit strengthen me to be more Christlike in my thoughts and actions. In Jesus' name. Amen.

Apostolic succession

FOR READING AND MEDITATION
JOHN 15:18–27

'… the Spirit of truth … will testify about me; but you
also must testify …' (vv.26–27)

We come now to the seventh step in the preparation
of the disciples to receive the Holy Spirit – the
teaching that the Holy Spirit would witness to Jesus
and would cause others to witness to Him also. After
the descent of the Spirit at Pentecost, the apostles said:
'We are witnesses of these things, and so is the Holy
Spirit, whom God has given to those who obey him'
(Acts 5:32). Here were human spirits and the Holy Spirit
working together for the same purpose – witnessing to
Jesus. The creative Spirit makes creative persons who
in turn go out and make other creative persons. This is
true apostolic succession, where we transmit not merely
truth but the Holy Spirit of truth Himself.

*O Creator Spirit, live within me and make me a creative
person so that I can go out and help make other people
creative. In Jesus' name. Amen.*

Stir yourself

'… *fan into flame the gift of God, which is in you through the laying on of my hands.*' (v.6)

P aul had laid his hands on Timothy and a gift of God had been imparted to him at that moment. Note, however, that a spiritual gift of this nature does not operate of its own accord – it needs the co-operation of the person concerned to bring it to full expression. 'Fan into flame the gift of God, which is in you' is Paul's strong advice. Permit me to ask you this personal question: What gifts has God imparted to you? If you are a Christian you will have some of God's gifts residing within you – at least one (see Rom. 12:6). What are you doing with that gift? Is it lying dormant within you? If so, don't wait for God to stir you – stir yourself. Fan it into flame. Now. Today.

O God, forgive me that so often I wait for You to stir me up when I ought to do it myself. Thank You for the gifts You have given me. I stir myself to go out and use them in Your name. Amen.

First things first

FOR READING AND MEDITATION
JAMES 5:7–19

*'Is anyone … sick? He should call the elders … to pray
over him and anoint him with oil …' (v.14)*

If we become seriously ill we should invite those we
know who have the Holy Spirit residing within them
to lay their hands upon us and ask God to heal us. This
does not mean, however, that we ought to ignore medical
opinion and think that to consult a doctor demonstrates
a lack of faith. *It is not a denial of God's power or a lack
of faith to consult a physician whenever you are ill.* God
uses physical as well as spiritual means to restore us to
health. Paul told Timothy to drink a little wine for his
stomach's sake (1 Tim. 5:23). But let's be careful that
in paying attention to the physical remedies that God
has built into His creation we do not ignore the spiritual
remedies as well.

*Gracious and loving heavenly Father, help me whenever I
fall sick to remind myself of all the remedies You have built
into the world to help me be well again. In Jesus' name.
Amen.*

Generation to regeneration

FOR READING AND MEDITATION
GENESIS 1:1–19

'Now the earth was formless and empty ... and the Spirit of God was hovering over the waters.' (v.2)

Wherever the Spirit is, there is creation. The energy that flows from the Holy Spirit is a creative energy. He was not only involved in the generation of the universe but He is the agent for regeneration also. He is the One who brings about the experience that we call 'the new birth'. But He is not content just to bring one soul to birth; He is desirous to co-operate with the other members of the Trinity in 'bringing *many* sons to glory' (Heb. 2:10). The creative Spirit makes creative persons who then, in turn, share their faith with others and, provided those others receive, then they too become creative persons. Evangelism is not complete until the evangelised become evangelists.

Holy Spirit, I sense that just as You hovered over creation You hover over my life too – longing to bring me up to my full maturity in Christ and reach others through me. Amen.

The overflow

FOR READING AND MEDITATION
I JOHN 4:1–21

'We are from God, and whoever knows God listens ...'
(v.6)

Would you like to be creative and contagious? Then be filled with the Spirit. The more full of the Spirit you are, the more you will transmit His energy and power to all with whom you come in contact. It is an unconscious operation, not a conscious one. You don't focus on transmitting it; you simply drink of the Spirit and let others drink of the overflow. If you are not full you don't have anything to give away. A humorist puts it like this: 'If a bishop hasn't the Spirit of God but has the measles and he lays his hands on you, you will not get the Spirit of God but you will get the measles.' Make sure that what you are giving flows from the Spirit.

Creator Spirit, dwell in me so rightly and powerfully that I will become a truly creative and contagious person. Fill me to overflowing. In Jesus' name. Amen.

The Spirit's tutelage

FOR READING AND MEDITATION
JOHN 16:1–16

'When he comes, he will convict the world of guilt in regard to sin and righteousness and judgment.' (v.8)

We look now at the eighth statement of the progressive teaching contained in John's Gospel concerning the coming of the Holy Spirit. The passage today points out the fact that when the Spirit comes He will convict of three things: 'guilt in regard to sin and righteousness and judgment'. Our consciences have a capacity to judge between right and wrong, but we put the content of what is right and wrong in by our imperfect training and upbringing. The apostle Paul had a conscience that was trained by the Holy Spirit. This is what he said in Romans 9:1: 'My conscience confirms it in the Holy Spirit.' His conscience was under the tutelage of the Spirit. So must ours be also.

Holy Spirit, cleanse my conscience from all that is imperfect and false. I want a conscience that is trained to approve what You approve and condemn what You condemn. Amen.

Facing central issues

FOR READING AND MEDITATION
1 JOHN 3:11–24

'This then is how … we set our hearts at rest in his presence whenever our hearts condemn us.' (vv.19–20)

There is a form of guilt that does not come down from God but up from within ourselves. True guilt is designed to help the personality, not hinder it. True guilt has been defined as God's way of saying: 'You have broken one of my principles.' False guilt destroys rather than builds up, and many suffer from incapacitating self-condemnation. False guilt arises when we condemn ourselves over issues where we have not been at fault. For example, a survivor of a plane crash can feel guilty they have escaped whilst others have perished. The conscience condemns us of both true and false guilt, which is why we need the illumination of the Holy Spirit to ensure our consciences function as they were designed to.

Father, I know Your love holds me and will not let me off when real guilt arises, but train my conscience so that I do not condemn myself with false guilt. Amen.

The core of sin

FOR READING AND MEDITATION
JOHN 15:9–27

'If I had not come and spoken to them, they would not be guilty of sin.' (v.22)

Here is a definition of sin from Jesus Himself that makes all other definitions secondary: Sin is 'not believing in Me'. The reality of sin is that we do not make Christ the centre of our lives, and we become the centre. In other words – we become God. Making ourselves God is the very essence of sin. Someone has described sin as 'anarchy'. The use of this word helps us understand even more clearly, perhaps, what sin is all about. Anarchy denies the right of a ruler to rule. When we live our lives with the ego at the centre instead of Christ then we are really saying to God: 'I want to run my life on my own terms.' There is no greater anarchy. For we are denying the right of the divine Ruler to rule.

O God, can it be that at times I live my life as an anarchist? Forgive me if this is so. Help me not to be an ego-centred person but a Christ-centred person. Amen.

'Let Me do the work'

FOR READING AND MEDITATION
ROMANS 3:9–31

'But now a righteousness from God, apart from law, has been made known …' (v.21)

ook at Jesus' words once again: 'When he comes [the Holy Spirit], he will convict the world … in regard to righteousness, because I am going to the Father' (John 16:8–10). Our Lord is talking here about the righteousness brought about by His sacrificial death – described so carefully and clearly by Paul – which only the Holy Spirit can reveal and apply to our hearts. Only the Holy Spirit can reveal to a person his or her need of righteousness. After I had left college to begin the work of the ministry, I foolishly thought I could show people their need of righteousness, but then the Spirit said to me: 'You provide the words, but let me do the work.'

Father, I see how releasing this fact can be – in my witnessing to You I provide the words, but You provide the power. Amen.

Christ's footprint

FOR READING AND MEDITATION
ROMANS 16:17–27

'The God of peace will soon crush Satan under your feet.'
(v.20)

Jesus said: 'When he comes [the Holy Spirit], he will convict the world ... *in regard to judgment, because the prince of this world now stands condemned'* (John 16:8,11). More than power is involved in the cross and resurrection. God acts in justice also, and at Calvary the ruler of this world – the very personification of evil – was effectively overthrown and judged. Making this news known and applying it to human hearts is also the work and ministry of the Holy Spirit. The cross would appear to many to be a triumph for Satan, but the Holy Spirit comes alongside and puts the whole thing into proper perspective. Christmas Evans said that on the back of the devil's neck is Christ's footprint.

Blessed Lord Jesus, I am so thankful that I face nothing that You have not faced and conquered. This gives me a glorious sense of victory as I go on in life. Amen.

The Spirit's humility

FOR READING AND MEDITATION
JOHN 16:12–33

'But when he, the Spirit of truth, comes, he will guide you into all truth.' (v.13)

The next lesson about the Holy Spirit that we come to in John's Gospel is the revelation that the Holy Spirit would guide into all truth. This goes a step beyond the stage we read about in John 14:26 where He was promised as a Teacher and a 'Remembrancer', and tells us that the Spirit would seek to ensure that not one permanent or fundamental principle or insight would be overlooked in the Spirit's ministry to the Church. The phrase 'he will not speak on his own … only what he hears' (v.13) makes clear that the Spirit will be under the complete supervision and direction of the Father and the Son. The Holy Spirit is co-equal with the Father and Son but humbly submits to them.

Blessed Holy Spirit, thank You for the part You played and still play in the purposes of redemption. Help me also to put the Father and Son ahead of any personal preference. Amen.

All truth

FOR READING AND MEDITATION
MATTHEW 17:1–13

'Peter said to Jesus, "Lord … If you wish, I will put up three shelters …"' (v.4)

As Christians we tend to focus on just part of all truth. We see an example of this tendency to camp alongside a single truth in our passage today. Peter was so thrilled and delighted to witness the transfiguration of the Lord that he wanted to build three tabernacles: one for Jesus, one for Moses and one for Elijah. Peter wanted to live in the realm where his feelings were stirred – the realm of inspiration. But there was a poor demon-possessed boy in the valley who needed deliverance. The inspiration on the mount needed now to be passed into demonstration. However gripping and inspirational any truth is, it must be balanced against other truths. It is not just truth we ought to be interested in – it is all truth.

Father, I want to know the truth, the whole truth and nothing but the truth. Curb the tendency within me that delights to focus on some truths and exclude others. In Jesus' name. Amen.

Know your Bible

FOR READING AND MEDITATION
2 TIMOTHY 2:11–26

'Do your best to present yourself to God as one ... who correctly handles the word of truth.' (v.15)

We continue meditating on the phrase 'the Spirit ... will guide you into all truth'. The best way of allowing the Holy Spirit to lead you into all truth is to soak your mind in the Scriptures. Those who say they are interested in knowing the truth about God but never read or study the Bible will never come to know the truth about Him. If our meditations about God are not based on Scripture, they will simply be human ideas about God. The Bible is God's revelation of Himself. The Holy Spirit promises to reveal all the truth we need to know about God, and the truth He reveals is always in harmony and accordance with the Word of God – the Scriptures.

Father, I see so clearly that the entrance of Your Word gives light and the neglecting of Your Word gives darkness. Let Your Holy Spirit be my Guide as I regularly explore the Bible. Amen.

A fatal flaw

FOR READING AND MEDITATION
2 TIMOTHY 3:1–17

'... the holy Scriptures ... are able to make you wise for salvation ...' (v.15)

Some say all truth is God's truth and we can combine the truths of the Bible and the truths of science. There is, however, a fatal flaw in this argument. How do we know the 'truth' of science is really truth? Years ago social scientists advocated the idea that we ought not to discipline children. Children develop better when they are allowed free expression, they said. This was supposed to be 'truth' borne out by empirical observation. Later, these ideas were discredited because people came to see that what looked like truth wasn't really truth at all. We must be very careful about mixing the 'truths' of the world with God's Word. The Bible is without error. The same cannot be said of natural science.

Father, I know that You reveal Yourself through nature, but that book is smudged and tainted by the Fall. Scripture, however, is not. Amen.

'Guides, not guideposts'

FOR READING AND MEDITATION
PSALM 25:1–22

'Guide me in your truth and teach me, for you are God my Saviour …' (v.5)

A Christian professor said: 'The biggest problem we have in America in relation to this issue is teaching people not just to be guideposts, but to be guides.' He meant that people in training are often content to learn the principles they need to tell people how to live, but do not put those principles into action themselves. Where this is so, the Holy Spirit is not fully in control. When He guides He shows us not only what the truth is, but also how to apply it to our lives. He takes us by the hand and seeks to turn the ideal into the real, aspiration into acceptance, and makes everything operate in the here and now. We are to become illustrations of divine truth in a way that others can observe and understand.

Holy Spirit, You are my Guide – help me to follow. Lead me not only into the understanding of truth but also into the possession of it such that I become an illustration of it. Amen.

What could He mean?

FOR READING AND MEDITATION
REVELATION 1:1–20

'Write, therefore, what you have seen, what is now and what will take place later.' (v.19)

The next lesson that Jesus taught the disciples in John's Gospel was that the Holy Spirit is to be prophetic: 'He will tell you what is yet to come' (John 16:13). You have only to pick up a Bible commentary to see that there is a variety of opinions as to the meaning of this phrase. But simply consider this – those who possess the Spirit will never be behind the times but always ahead of the times. Having the eternal Spirit gives us deeper insight not only into the past or the present but into the future also.

Father, I know one thing for sure – I may not know everything the future holds but I know who holds the future. Help me lay hold of this certain knowledge, in Jesus' name I pray. Amen.

Director of Publishing

FOR READING AND MEDITATION
2 PETER 1:1-21

'... men spoke from God as they were carried along by the Holy Spirit.' (v.21)

We are all aware that the Holy Spirit was closely involved in the writing and compilation of the Old Testament. This is made crystal clear in our passage today. But He was closely involved in the writing and compilation of the New Testament also. Just think what a Director of Publishing the Holy Spirit is. He has pulled together the one and only published work of God and given us in a single volume all we need to know about how to live for Him in this world and prepare for the world that is to come. The Holy Spirit played a major part in the compilation of both Testaments, but I venture to suggest it was not the writing of the New Testament that Jesus had in mind when He said: 'He will tell you what is yet to come.'

Father, You inspired the Scriptures and only You can correctly interpret them. I am grateful. Amen.

Predicting the future

FOR READING AND MEDITATION
REVELATION 19:1–21

'Worship God! For the testimony of Jesus is the spirit of prophecy.' (v.10)

We are considering how the Holy Spirit will tell us what is yet to come. One school of thought suggests that there are two ways to tell the future – one is by foresight and the other is by insight. When people predict the future by foresight, they impose their declaration upon the events. When a person predicts the future by insight, he or she is aware that certain ways fit in with God's way and forecasts the future by the present. An example of prediction by foresight would be the foretelling of the Gulf War before it happened. An example of prediction by insight would be the affirmation that any system that does not have upon it the stamp and character of Jesus Christ cannot possibly prevail.

Lord, support me, I pray, as I move forward, thinking through these deep and profound words that fell from Your lips. Others can give me argument, but only You can give me understanding. Amen.

The final word

FOR READING AND MEDITATION
1 JOHN 2:1–17

'... the man who does the will of God lives for ever.'
(v.17)

Commenting on Revelation 19:10, Dr E.S. Jones said: 'If you testify to Jesus and point men to Jesus as having the final word, then you have the spirit of prophecy. You are forecasting the future, for you see the present. The way of Jesus is the Way – the Way unqualified ... every other way is not-the-way.' The point he is making is that as Christians we can write the destiny of everything and we can write it now because we know that the way of Jesus will be the way in which everything will turn out in the end. I love these ideas but they are not, I believe, what Jesus had in mind when He said: 'He will tell you what is yet to come.'

O Father, I am thrilled to see even more clearly that in You the past, present and future are unfolded. Help me, then, to boldly proclaim the final victory even though it is not here. Amen.

JUNE 20

The Spirit predicts

FOR READING AND MEDITATION
ACTS 21:1–16

'Through the Spirit they urged Paul not to go on to Jerusalem.' (v.4)

S o what did Jesus really mean when He said: 'He
will tell you what is yet to come'? I think He meant
exactly what He said – the Holy Spirit would unfold for
us certain future events. There is no doubt in my mind
that the Holy Spirit who revealed some of the facts about
the future to those who were in the Early Church (Acts
11:27–30) wants to be at work in the same way in today's
Church. I know that predictive prophecy is frowned upon
in certain sections of the Christian community, but there
is no evidence to suggest that the prophetic nature of
the Spirit's work ceased after the Acts of the Apostles.
We need both openness and discernment to receive of
the Spirit whilst avoiding error.

*Holy Spirit, You who know the past, present and future, let
not our doubts and fears hinder You from being at work
in Your Church. Where things about the future need to be
revealed then show us. Amen.*

Continued humiliation

FOR READING AND MEDITATION
PHILIPPIANS 2:1–11

'... he humbled himself and became obedient to death
– even death on a cross!' (v.8)

The eleventh lesson is that the end result of the coming of the Spirit is not to glorify the disciples but to glorify Jesus. This is how our Lord put it: 'He [the Holy Spirit] will bring glory to me ...' (John 16:14). These words, spoken in the process of educating the disciples to receive the Spirit, point to the ultimate purpose of the coming of the Spirit. The Son of God experienced the deepest humiliation possible – exchanging the throne of God for a carpenter's bench. But that was not all – there was further and deeper humiliation as He moved through life, being ridiculed, mocked, ostracised and finally strung up on a cross to die. Is it any wonder that the Spirit delights to glorify Jesus?

Holy Spirit, thank You for the work You have done in my life, and indeed continue to do, by focusing my attention on Jesus. Just as You delight in Him – so do I. Amen.

Whose is the glory?

'Worthy is the Lamb who was slain, to receive power and wealth and wisdom and strength …' (v.12)

Many years ago I witnessed a young man saved from drowning in the sea off the Welsh coast. A lifeguard ran into the sea, swam out to where he was – a distance of several hundred yards – and saved him from what would no doubt have been certain death. Artificial respiration had to be given for a while, but eventually the man recovered and all was well. I noticed, however, that when the excitement was over, the crowd lingered not around the man who had been saved but around the one who had saved him. I felt rather sorry for the man who had been rescued, and I watched him as he walked off on his own. Then a thought stirred within me that I have never forgotten. The glory goes to the one who saves.

O Spirit of God, focus my eyes on Jesus so that I glance at other things but gaze only on Him. In Him I find all the fullness of the Godhead, and in praising Him I praise the whole Trinity. Amen.

'Lighting up His face'

FOR READING AND MEDITATION
I CORINTHIANS 12:1–11

'... no one can say, "Jesus is Lord," except by the Holy Spirit.' (v.3)

The reason why Jesus is continually glorified is because He is the One who has revealed God, and therefore when He is glorified we can see exactly who is being glorified. One time when I was in India the taxi in which I was travelling was caught up in some heavy traffic and brought to a halt. As we waited, we saw a marriage procession in which a bridegroom, riding on a white horse, was being escorted to meet his bride. The friends and relatives of the bridegroom, who were walking alongside, had torches that they held up to illuminate the face of the bridegroom for all to see. A friend who was with me said: 'The work of the Holy Spirit is like that. He comes to light up the face of Jesus.' He does!

Blessed Holy Spirit, give me a clear vision of Jesus so that He will be my constant focus. For I long that everything I do and everything I decide shall be according to Him. Amen.

Our objective standard

FOR READING AND MEDITATION
HEBREWS 12:1–13

'Let us fix our eyes on Jesus, the author and perfecter of our faith ...' (v.2)

One of the greatest temptations we face in the Christian life is to go off on a tangent as regards subjectivity. Let me explain what I mean. It is perilously possible for our unconscious mind to give suggestions to the conscious mind that we may interpret as the voice of the Spirit. A Christian young woman heard a voice inside her head telling her it was right to take vengeance on someone who had criticised her Christian stand. She thought it was the Spirit, but it was nothing more than a subconscious desire. Vengeance is not according to the Spirit of Jesus. Everything has to be tested as to whether it fits into Jesus – our objective standard.

Father, I see that things can go on inside me that are so easy for me to misinterpret. That is why I am so glad to know that I have a safe test for everything. It must be according to Jesus. Amen.

The ultimate safeguard

FOR READING AND MEDITATION
ACTS 2:14–28

'David said … "I saw the Lord always before me."' (v.25)

We conclude our meditation on the eleventh lesson in the 'School of the Spirit' by focusing on the words 'He will bring glory to me *by taking from what is mine and making it known to you*' (John 16:14, my italics). The parameters within which the Spirit works when applying redemption are fixed in Christ. Every truth or fact we need to know about how to live effectively for God on this earth has been displayed and demonstrated in Jesus, and the Spirit works to apply those truths and facts to our hearts. If at any time we doubt whether the Spirit is leading us, we can say to ourselves: 'Is what I am being led into in harmony with the Spirit of Jesus?' If it is then you are safe. Jesus is the ultimate safeguard.

Father, You have given me in Jesus the ultimate safeguard for my life. Draw me closer to Him so that His thoughts become my thoughts, His desires my desires, and His will my will. Amen.

'Take the Holy Spirit'

FOR READING AND MEDITATION
JOHN 20:19–31

*'And ... he breathed on them and said, "Receive the Holy
Spirit."'* (v.22)

We come now to the last lesson in the Gospel of
John that Jesus gave to His disciples concerning
the Holy Spirit. The whole purpose of the previous eleven
steps was to bring them to this – the receiving of the
Spirit as a personal gift. The quest ended in finding. My
purpose in these final days of our meditations on this
subject is not to go into a detailed exposition of this
particular text but to focus on the fact that *the whole
purpose of the Holy Spirit being given is that we might
receive*. The end of the learning for the disciples was the
creation of a yearning that became receptivity, which
became finding. This is also how it must be with us.

*O Father, I yearn for more of You and Your Spirit. May I
have a greater awareness of Your Spirit's presence in my
heart and a greater increase of divine power than I have
known before. Amen.*

Keep on being filled

FOR READING AND MEDITATION
EPHESIANS 5:1–21

'… be filled with the Spirit.' (v.18)

O ur text for today tells us that it is not enough to be filled; we must keep on being filled. That is the plain meaning of this particular scripture. The late Dr Handley Moule, a bishop in the Church of England, said: 'The difference between a soul filled and one that is unfilled is the difference between a well in which there is a spring of water choked and a well in which the obstruction is removed so that the water springs up and fills the well.' Ask yourself now: Is there anything choking the spring of water that God put within me? Resentments, fears, self-centredness, and the like? How thirsty are you for God? Jesus said: 'If a man is thirsty, let him come to me and drink' (John 7:37).

My Father and my God, I want to live in the strength and energy of the Spirit, to be full of poise and full of power. Take all of me and put me under Your control. In Jesus' name. Amen.

'Hot pots' and 'cold pots'

FOR READING AND MEDITATION
2 TIMOTHY 1:1–18

'For God did not give us a spirit of timidity, but a spirit of power …' (v.7)

Some are afraid that if they open up to the Spirit they might become a 'hot pot'. Believe me, the danger to the Church is not from 'hot pots' but from 'cold pots'. I tell you that fear comes from the devil himself and has probably kept more Christians away from opening their beings to the Holy Spirit than any other thing. Let me quote you these words of Jesus: 'Which of you fathers, if your son asks for a fish, will give him a snake instead? Or if he asks for an egg, will give him a scorpion?' (Luke 11:11–12). God is infinitely more loving than the most affectionate of earthly fathers, and you can take it on the Master's authority that when you ask for the Holy Spirit, that is what you will receive.

Father, grant that all my fears might at this very moment give way to faith. I can't trust myself, but I don't have to – I can trust You. I believe. Amen.

The key to receiving

FOR READING AND MEDITATION
JOHN 12:12–33

'… the man who hates his life in this world will keep it for eternal life.' (v.25)

How, then, do we receive the Spirit, or, if you prefer, *more* of the Spirit? It can all be explained in one simple word – surrender. By surrender I mean the surrender of ourselves, the central fundamental self, not merely 'things'. It is possible to surrender your money, your possessions and everything you own without surrendering yourself. I have known people who said they had surrendered their 'all' to God but kept the self – indeed even asserted the self. The attitude that leads to receiving more of the Spirit is always that of receptivity to God. When the self is in the right place – the place of surrender – then anything can happen. And usually it does!

Father, I am thankful that You are uncovering my ego, not to humiliate and shame me, but to lift me. Right now I surrender my ego into Your hands. You are mine and I am Yours – for ever. Amen.

Amazing self-surrender

FOR READING AND MEDITATION
ACTS 2:1–21

'All of them were filled with the Holy Spirit …' (v.4)

When God offers His highest gift, which is the Holy Spirit – an amazing self-surrender to us, by the way – then of necessity He must demand a self-surrender from us. For without self-surrender we would use this new-found power in the service of the self. But how do I surrender, you ask? I suggest – on your knees. Not that the physical position is all that important but I have found there is something about getting on one's knees in God's presence that aids the soul. You have travelled a long way with me over these past weeks. The lessons are now over. It's time for the test. Lay aside all your preconceived ideas and open your being to the life of God. Say it with a meaning greater than ever before – come, Holy Spirit, come!

Holy Spirit, how can I sufficiently thank You for giving Yourself to me? Now I give myself to You – wholly and entirely. Spirit of the living God, fall afresh on me. In Jesus' name. Amen.

I belong

FOR READING AND MEDITATION
MATTHEW 1:1–17

*'Boaz was the father of Obed, whose mother was Ruth
…' (v.5)*

O ur theme for the next two months centres on the only two books in the Bible that are named after women – Esther and Ruth. We focus first on the story of Ruth. The first thing we must notice about Ruth is that her name is included in Matthew's genealogy of our Lord Jesus Christ. Good and godly though Ruth was, however, the real reason her name is mentioned here is because she was among those who were the direct antecedents of the Lord Jesus Christ. She and the others are given prominence not because of what they had achieved but because of whom they were related to – Jesus. This is where real significance lies – *in being related to Him*. Never forget you are who you are because He is who He is.

O Father, how can I ever thank You enough for bringing me into a relationship with Yourself and with Your Son? I belong – belong to You and thus to everyone else who belongs to You. Amen.

Spiritual dryness

FOR READING AND MEDITATION
JUDGES 17:1–13

'In those days Israel had no king; everyone did as he saw fit.' (v.6)

Ruth arrived on the scene in the period when the judges ruled in Israel. The children of Israel had occupied the land for some time. But the peace and prosperity that had been theirs disappeared after Joshua's death, when the people returned to their evil and disobedient ways. The condition of Israel at the time Ruth appears was, as our text for today points out, that 'everyone did as he saw fit'. As a direct consequence of this rebellion there was famine in the land – physical and spiritual. When men and women turn from God and persist in doing what is right in their own eyes, barrenness and dryness follow – as surely as night follows day.

O God, I know that Your way always leads to fruitfulness. In the hour of spiritual dryness help me to track down its cause and then turn to the cure – real and radical repentance. Amen.

The danger of expediency

FOR READING AND MEDITATION
RUTH 1:1–2

'A man ... together with his wife and two sons, went to live ... in the country of Moab.' (v.1)

Elimelech's decision to move his family into Moab may have appeared to be a good choice economically, but I believe it was a bad choice spiritually. He went directly against God's commands. It can be argued that when one considers the positive things that came out of the move then what they did was right. But when we see good coming out of something, we must never assume that God willed it that way; rather, He works through the bad to make all things contribute to His glory. Christians should make decisions on the basis of God's will as displayed in His Word. We live dangerously when we allow expediency, and not the clear guidelines of Scripture, to determine our actions and our directions.

O Father, burn into my consciousness the things I have read today so that I will never be directed by expediency but by the clear directions that come out of Your Word. Amen.

Putting God first

FOR READING AND MEDITATION
RUTH 1:3–5

'Now Elimelech, Naomi's husband, died, and she was left with her two sons.' (v.3)

Today's reading reinforces the point we made yesterday about the folly of making decisions based on expediency rather than on the will of God. A change of circumstances will not necessarily solve our problems. We think if we had a new home, a new church, a new husband or wife, a new minister, or a new job, that all our difficulties would be over. How prone we are to allow materialistic, personal or economic values to influence our judgment. As Christians, every major decision we make ought to be set against God's perfect will. We owe it to God to bring Him into our decision-making. Otherwise we may find we have gained economically but lost out spiritually.

Father, help me never to allow economic or personal considerations to influence my judgment when making life's major decisions. May I subject all my decisions to Your perfect will. Amen.

Forgive yourself!

FOR READING AND MEDITATION
RUTH 1:6–13

'Naomi and her daughters-in-law prepared to return home ...' (v.6)

N aomi seems overwhelmed by all that has happened and says: 'It is more bitter for me than for you, because the Lord's hand has gone out against me' (v.13). I cannot help but feel that there were some feelings of self-recrimination and self-contempt beneath that remark. Naomi, being an Israelite, would have known how to approach God for forgiveness. However, it would appear from the remark she makes that she has not yet forgiven herself. Self-pity and self-contempt are always signals that say one has not really received the divine forgiveness. Whenever you are in need of forgiveness, open your soul to receive it, and then make sure you do not short-circuit the spiritual system by failing to forgive yourself.

Father, I see how easy it is to allow sorrow for my sin to become self-reproach or self-pity. Help me, whenever I am in need of forgiveness, to receive it from You, and then to forgive myself. Amen.

The leap of faith

FOR READING AND MEDITATION
RUTH 1:14–18

'Where you go I will go, and where you stay I will stay.'
(v.16)

Ruth is well aware that great problems will face her when she arrives in Israel – national, cultural and religious – but she determines that nothing will dissuade her and cause her to turn back. What a magnificent picture this is of a true conversion. Ruth and Orpah stand at the crossroads. Orpah draws back to end her days in the darkness of heathen idolatry, while Ruth moves on to a new land and a new future, and to have her name inscribed forever on the sacred record. How sad that so many can appear to be deeply religious, travel for a time with God's people, yet fail to make that 'leap of faith' that entrusts all one has and all one is to the Saviour. If you have not done so, make the leap of faith today.

Gracious and loving Father, help me understand that keeping company with Your people is not enough for salvation. I must make that determined leap of faith. I do so now. In Jesus' name. Amen.

The marks of disobedience

FOR READING AND MEDITATION
RUTH 1:19–22

'The LORD has afflicted me; the Almighty has brought misfortune upon me.' (v.21)

I have met many in my time who stepped out of the will of God, and although they returned to Him and were forgiven, they still carry in their bodies and personalities the consequences of their actions. Naomi's words are still tinged with self-recrimination: 'Don't call me Naomi [sweet or pleasant] … Call me Mara [unpleasant] because the Almighty has made my life very bitter.' Naomi was a living testimony of what happens to those who choose some way other than God's way. 'Those who take God's way,' says Dr E. Stanley Jones, 'get results. Those who don't, get consequences.' The sin in which we engage can be forgiven, but the marks of sin may remain in us and upon us for a lifetime.

Father, I see that in this world I can either get results – or consequences. Help me not to go against the grain of the universe, for life is designed to move in one way – Your way. Amen.

Maximising time

FOR READING AND MEDITATION
RUTH 2:1–2

'Naomi had a relative on her husband's side ... a man of standing, whose name was Boaz.' (v.1)

Naomi came from a wealthy family but Ruth was a hard worker. In most cases, where God appeared to people [in the Bible] and called them to special service they were already busily engaged in some task. Moses was tending the sheep. Peter, James, John and Andrew were called to Christ's service when mending their nets. Some idly sit around waiting for God to call them to special service and wonder why they never hear His voice. God is looking to see how we are handling the ordinary tasks of life before He entrusts us with the special things. Put your whole energy into every task that comes your way and perhaps God will give you the opportunity to do bigger and greater things.

My Father and my God, help me see that the little tasks, when done well, qualify me for the bigger tasks that may be up ahead. May I turn to today's duties with enthusiasm and dedication. Amen.

Unconscious guidance

FOR READING AND MEDITATION
RUTH 2:2–3

'So she went out and began to glean in the fields behind the harvesters.' (v.3)

When the workers went through the fields reaping the harvest, often, because of the speed at which they worked, they would leave behind small unreaped sections. These areas were then covered by 'gleaners'. Jewish law stated that the gleanings must be left for the poor (Lev. 19:9–10; Deut. 24:19). As Ruth takes up the role of gleaner, she happens to find herself reaping in one of the fields that belonged to Boaz. The term used in the second half of our text for today, 'as it turned out', is filled with deep spiritual meaning. Divine guidance was at work here. Ruth might not have realised it or sensed it, for most divine guidance takes place when we are not conscious of it.

Father, forgive me when I have thought things have happened to me because of luck, when really it has been You. How glad I am that I am being guided not by the stars but by the Saviour. Amen.

Nothing too trivial

FOR READING AND MEDITATION
RUTH 2:3

'As it turned out, she found herself working in a field belonging to Boaz ...' (v.3)

How reassuring it is to know that even when we are not seeking guidance, God is guiding us still. The world explains these things as coincidences, and sometimes they are no more than that, but there are also God-instances. God not only has a general providence – one in which all His creation benefits – but a special providence that involves only those who have a personal relationship with Him through His Son Jesus Christ (Rom. 8:28). After a lifetime of knowing God's special providence, the great Samuel Chadwick, one-time Principal of Cliff College in Derbyshire, England, said: 'The divine attention to detail is amazing. Nothing is too trivial for Omnipotence.'

O Father, how humbling yet how encouraging it is to know that You guide me even when I am not conscious of it. Thank You, dear Father. Thank You. Amen.

Management–labour relations

FOR READING AND MEDITATION
RUTH 2:4

*'Boaz … greeted the harvesters, "The LORD be with you!"
"The LORD bless you!" they called back.' (v.4)*

The secret of good employer–employee relations is for management to be caring, fair minded and honest, and workers to put in a good day's work. And where there is a Christian commitment on both sides then it adds great weight to the qualities I have mentioned. A leading industrialist in Pusan, Korea, told me during my visit there that before he found Christ the relationships between him and his workers were in turmoil. After he found Christ, he saw his employees in a new light. 'I worked out ways of how I could bless them,' he said, 'and they in turn worked out ways by which they could bless me.' When godliness prevails in a nation, one of the first things to be affected is management–labour relations.

Father, lay Your healing hand on the turmoil that is in so much of the relations between employers and employees. May everyone be concerned for the welfare of others. Amen.

Under His wings

FOR READING AND MEDITATION
RUTH 2:5–12

'May you be richly rewarded by the LORD … under whose wings you have come to take refuge.' (v.12)

Boaz already knows of the return of Naomi and how her daughter-in-law Ruth has stayed at her side. He sums up his feelings in the words: 'May the LORD repay you for what you have done. May you be richly rewarded by the LORD, the God of Israel, under whose wings you have come to take refuge' (v.12). Some of you have stood for God despite great criticism from your families and friends. He has seen all your tears, all your heartache and all your sacrifices. And He promises you a perfect reward one day. Draw close to Him now and nestle beneath the shelter of His great wings. Look up and see how easily they cover you. Under His wings there is no further need for tears – just trust!

Father, how marvellous is Your timing. Just when I need it, You find a way of bringing me the greatest encouragement. When all other doors are closed, You find a secret stair into my soul. Amen.

Handfuls – on purpose

FOR READING AND MEDITATION
RUTH 2:13–17

'... pull out some stalks for her from the bundles and
leave them for her to pick up ...' (v.16)

Once Ruth has completed her meal, she returns
to her gleaning. Yet again, Boaz intervenes on
her behalf by instructing his servants to let fall whole
handfuls of grain so that she has plenty to gather. I love
the way the Amplified Bible describes this moment: 'And
let fall some handfuls for her on purpose.' 'Handfuls ...
on purpose.' What a beautiful expression. It is a picture
of how God goes before each one of His toiling servants
and lets fall 'handfuls on purpose' – some tokens of His
goodness, some special encouragement, some evidence
of His care, that serves to keep us moving forward and
keep our hearts bent on the divine task. How gracious
and loving is our Lord.

O Father, how easy it is to remember the discouragements
and forget the encouragements. Forgive me for my proneness
to do this. Thank You for every 'handful on purpose' that
comes my way. Amen.

On looking back

FOR READING AND MEDITATION
RUTH 2:18–21

'The LORD … has not stopped showing his kindness to the living and the dead.' (v.20)

Ruth returns to report on the events of the day with a whole ephah of barley. An ephah is no small measure. In today's terms it is about half a bushel, or nearly ten kilos. Together, Ruth and Naomi look back over the day and give thanks to God for the evidence of His guiding hand. Naomi's joy knows no bounds because she senses that Ruth's meeting with Boaz has a providential feel about it. Boaz was a close relative who had the right to redeem Ruth and take her to be his wife. They find, as you and I have found, that the evidences of the divine design are certainly there as we look back.

Father, I am better at looking back and thanking You than I am at looking ahead and praising You. Help me learn from what I have experienced of Your guiding hand to trust You more in the future. Amen.

If only we believed

FOR READING AND MEDITATION
RUTH 2:22–23

'Ruth stayed close to the servant girls ... until the barley
and wheat harvests were finished.' (v.23)

Like Naomi, each one of us must recognise that in
the ebb and flow of life's circumstances, an eternal
God is quietly pursuing His purposes. Little, if anything,
happens by chance in the God-ordained life. He is there
in every emergency or situation that arises. When
you become aware that in the life of every one of His
children God is bent on bringing to pass His perfect
purposes, then although our anxieties and fears may
not be eliminated, they are certainly reduced. If only we
could grasp the truth of Romans 8:28: 'All things work
together for good' (AV) then hardly a fear would arise
in our hearts. Our trouble is not that we do not believe
God's word; our trouble is we do not believe it enough.

*My Father and my God, grant that Your word might move
from my intellect right into my heart. I don't want just to
hold Your word; I want it to hold me. Amen.*

A budding romance

FOR READING AND MEDITATION
RUTH 3:1

'My daughter, should I not try to find a home for you …?'
(v.1)

As Naomi ponders the sovereignty of God in the meeting between Ruth and Boaz, she begins to realise there is a distinct possibility that Boaz will take on the responsibility of marrying Ruth and providing the security she needs in the future. She begins, therefore, to formulate a clear and daring plan to ensure the continuance of the budding romance. Note how she opens up the conversation: 'My daughter, should I not try to find a home for you, where you will be well provided for? Is not Boaz … a kinsman of ours?' (vv.1–2). This is not meddling or matchmaking, but simply bringing her thoughts and responses to bear on the issues that God has opened up to her own insight.

Father, help me to understand Your purposes and how I should bring my own thoughts and responses to bear on the issues so I can walk through the doors of opportunity You open for me. Amen.

Three pieces of advice

FOR READING AND MEDITATION
RUTH 3:2–5

'Ruth … went down to the threshing-floor and did everything her mother-in-law told her to do.' (v.5)

During the time of the winnowing of the grain, it was customary for the workers to sleep on the threshing-floor. Naomi's carefully formulated plan was designed to work precisely at this point. What a delightful picture this gives us of the relationship that exists between each one of us and our Lord Jesus Christ. Just as Ruth was within her legal rights in approaching Boaz as a male relative, so we, as God's children, have a legal right to approach the throne of grace and avail ourselves of God's provision. We must be careful, however, that we do not mistake a need for a want. God is not under an obligation to give us everything we want, but He is under an obligation to give us everything we need.

Father, the thought that I have a legal right to approach Your throne and claim Your provision for my needs is awesome. Help me to appropriate the rich inheritance I have in Christ. Amen.

A binding contract

FOR READING AND MEDITATION
RUTH 3:8–9

'Spread the corner of your garment over me, since you are a kinsman-redeemer.' (v.9)

By this simple custom of lying at Boaz's feet Ruth was really saying: 'I belong to you and I want you to take care of me.' The custom of covering a bride with a tallith, or fringed garment (Ezek. 16:8), is still part of Jewish matrimonial ritual to this day. What spiritual lesson can be drawn from this beautiful and inspiring picture of Ruth lying at Boaz's feet? This – the Church, though surrounded at this present moment by a deep and dense darkness, is nevertheless resting safely and securely at the Saviour's feet. But this is not all. His covering of us by the robe of righteousness is also the pledge that one day He is going to join us to Himself in a marriage that will last for all eternity.

O Father, just to live with You in eternity would have been enough to delight my soul for ever, but to be joined to You, to be one with You, to be part of Your Bride, is more than I deserve. Amen.

A problem

FOR READING AND MEDITATION
RUTH 3:10–13

'Although it is true that I am near of kin, there is a kinsman-redeemer nearer than I.' (v.12)

One problem faces the couple as they contemplate marriage. There is a closer relative than Boaz. Jewish law specifically required the next of kin, if he was single, to take on the responsibility of marrying a widow, but Boaz is second in line. He vows before the Lord that he will seek a settlement of the matter as quickly as possible, and then encourages Ruth to rest comfortably and contentedly until the morning. If there was a kinsman nearer than Boaz then why did not Ruth present herself to him? The answer will become clear as we reach the end of the story. For the moment, let it be enough to recognise in this the guiding and planning of the Almighty.

Father, give me, I pray, an ever-increasing consciousness of the wonder of divine guidance. Let the fact that 'nothing is too trivial for Omnipotence' continually amaze and astonish me. Amen.

Wait!

FOR READING AND MEDITATION
RUTH 3:14–17

'"Bring me the shawl you are wearing ... " he poured into it six measures of barley.' (v.15)

When Ruth finally reports to Naomi all that has happened in the night, and particularly the fact that there is a kinsman nearer than Boaz, Naomi gives her this advice: 'Wait ... For the man will not rest until the matter is settled today' (v.18). It is not easy to wait, especially where matters of the heart are concerned. But no Christian is mature until he or she has learned to wait. Are you feeling spiritually restless at the moment, straining at a spiritual leash? A purpose far wiser than you can ever conceive of is being worked out for you. A heart infinitely more loving than any other you will ever know is caring for you. A mind greater than yours is planning for you. So – wait!

Father, forgive me that so often I move ahead when I should wait, and rush around when I should be standing still. Teach me the art of waiting. In Jesus' name I pray. Amen.

Confident trust

FOR READING AND MEDITATION
RUTH 3:18

'... the man will not rest until the matter is settled today.'
(v.18)

Who can fail to see in these words a picture of Christ, our heavenly Boaz, who at the beginning of time set about the task of overcoming every obstacle that stood in the way of our salvation? Such was His commitment to us that He endured the most horrifying experiences to woo us, and win us to Himself. I am reminded of an old preacher who was expounding the difficulties that Christ overcame in order to bring us safely to heaven. He put it in this quaint but intriguing way: 'God thought it, Christ bought it, the Holy Spirit wrought it – thank God I've got it!' With all my heart I say – Amen!

Gracious and loving Father, when I contemplate the tremendous obstacles and difficulties that my Lord Jesus Christ overcame to save me, there are just no words to express my gratitude. Amen.

Three conditions

FOR READING AND MEDITATION
RUTH 4:1

'When the kinsman-redeemer ... came along, Boaz said,
"Come over here, my friend, and sit down."' (v.1)

What does the term 'kinsman-redeemer' mean? The word 'redeem' means 'to buy back' or 'set free'. It is the act by which a person's property or liberty is purchased through the payment of a special price. A kinsman-redeemer was someone who became involved in buying the rights and privileges of another family member. As such, several things were required of him. First, he must be a near kinsman, related by birth (Lev. 25:47–49). Second, he must be able to pay the required price. Third, he must enter into any agreement willingly and without coercion. All three of these conditions Boaz was able to meet. My mind flies, as I write, to another Kinsman-Redeemer, whose name is Jesus, who met these three same conditions.

Lord Jesus Christ, You joined Yourself to the human race in the Incarnation, paid for my redemption with Your own life on the cross, and did all of this freely out of love. Amen.

A temporary setback

FOR READING AND MEDITATION
RUTH 4:2–4

'"If you will redeem [the land], do so." ... "I will redeem it," he said.' (v.4)

If the nearest relative bought the dead man's land, Jewish law stated that he then had legal rights over the family. Should this happen now, Boaz would not be able to claim Ruth as his wife. Some might have turned away at this stage but not Boaz. In his heart burned a love that would not be dampened by difficulties. This is the wonderful thing about true love – it leaps over all obstacles, opposes every argument, and moves on relentlessly until it possesses the object of its affection and makes it its own. Our Saviour's love was of this kind also – but of course infinitely greater. He has argued the case on our behalf and won! Now we find ourselves belonging to Him – for ever.

O loving Saviour, how can I sufficiently thank You for pleading my case in the courts of heaven and winning on the cross my eternal freedom and redemption? I love You Lord Jesus. Amen.

Persistence

FOR READING AND MEDITATION
RUTH 4:5–6

'… the kinsman-redeemer said … "I might endanger my
own estate. You redeem it yourself."' (v.6)

How similar is all this to the torturous process
through which our Lord went in order to redeem
us. Our Lord, too, was presented with a great problem as
He set out to save us, for we were 'sold under sin' (Rom.
7:14, AV). We were slaves to the kingdom of Satan; we
belonged by right to him. Christ, however, came up with
a plan that enabled us to pass from the kingdom of Satan
into the kingdom of God. Satan thought he had us in his
clutches for all time but he was outmanoeuvred at the
cross. Just as Boaz persisted to overcome the kinsman
at Bethlehem, so our Lord persisted to overcome Satan
at Calvary. What the devil thought would be a great
victory turned out to be his most ignominious defeat.
Hallelujah!

O Father, when I reflect on with what deftness and skill You
overturned the strategies of Satan, I just want to open up
my heart to You in endless praise. Blessed be Your name for
ever. Amen.

The redemption ceremony

FOR READING AND MEDITATION
RUTH 4:7–8

'… for the redemption … to become final, one party took
off his sandal and gave it to the other.' (v.7)

Ruth's redemption was achieved publicly. Paul says
when speaking of our redemption: '… it was not
done in a corner' (Acts 26:26). He meant by this that
our Lord was not put to death in one of the back streets
of Jerusalem, away from the eyes of the multitudes, but
was crucified on a hill for all to see. There was a divine
purpose behind this. If Christ had died at the hand of an
assassin in some quiet corner of the city then His death
would have exposed the evil of only one man – a criminal
type of individual. The fact that Christ was officially and
publicly put to death meant that their condemnation
of Him was representative of the wishes of the whole
human race and witnessed by them.

*Father, I see that the cross exposes not just the sins of a few
but the sins of all humanity. But men did not take Your
life away from You; You laid it down of Yourself. I am so
grateful. Amen.*

Sealed and certified

FOR READING AND MEDITATION
RUTH 4:9–10

'Then Boaz announced to the elders and all the people,
"Today you are witnesses ..."' (v.9)

Boaz begins and ends his statement with these
words: 'Today you are witnesses.' Boaz wanted
to be sure that the transaction would never be called
into question in the future. People might be tempted to
query the legality of this at some later stage if not now
clearly sealed, settled and certified. For a similar reason,
our Lord's death was enacted before many witnesses.
As Christ was destined to rise from the dead a few days
afterwards, it was necessary that He be known to have
risen from the dead. People could easily have said: 'He did
not really die.' But He did die. His death was certified by
many witnesses. He had a certified death and therefore
an undeniable resurrection.

O Father, the more I see the depth of thought and the
attention to detail that went into the securing of my
redemption, the more thankful and humbled I feel. What a
salvation! What a Saviour! Amen.

A new identity

FOR READING AND MEDITATION
RUTH 4:11–12

*'Then the elders ... said ... "May the Lord make [Ruth]
... like Rachel and Leah ..."' (v.11)*

Rachel was highly regarded by the Jews. It seems
strange that the elders should wish for Ruth to
become as honoured and revered as Rachel, especially
when we remember that Ruth was a Moabitess, born
in a land that was under God's curse. What was it that
produced this strange turn of events? By linking himself
to Ruth, Boaz brought about a change in her identity and
this, of course, was recognised by all. This is precisely
what Christ has done for us. Though we were classified
as 'objects of wrath' and 'excluded from citizenship in
Israel and foreigners to the covenants of the promise ...'
(Eph. 2:3,12), Christ has joined Himself to us and given
us His own identity. We are no longer aliens – we belong
to Him.

*O God, how can I ever praise You enough for plucking me
out of the world and giving me a new heart, a new identity,
and one day a new name? Eternal praise and glory be to
You. Amen.*

A place in history

FOR READING AND MEDITATION
RUTH 4:11–12

'May you have standing in Ephratah and be famous in
Bethlehem.' (v.11)

I n due course, a son was born named Obed who in turn
had a son called Jesse. From Jesse came David. When
we trace the line of Ruth, we come to Matthew chapter 1
where she is listed alongside the others who were part
of our Lord's genealogy. Ruth's name, being included
in our Lord's line of descent, is stamped with a dignity
that even Rachel never had! It is almost impossible to
think of Bethlehem without thinking of King David. And
the great-grandmother of David was Ruth. The blessing
given by the elders turned out to be more than a blessing;
it was a prophecy. Ruth has become as well known in
Israel as Rachel and Leah, and her standing is as solid
and immovable as that of the city of Bethlehem.

*Father, the more I follow the story of Ruth, the more
convinced I am that Your sovereign purposes are at work
even when nothing seems to go right. Amen.*

Reflected glory

FOR READING AND MEDITATION
RUTH 4:13

'So Boaz took Ruth and she became his wife.' (v.13)

Immediately prior to the marriage, Ruth seems to be very much in the background. This is, after all, the story of a Moabitess, a penniless widow over whom hung a curse, finding favour and salvation through the intervention of another. The law of Israel barred Ruth's way to happiness and prosperity until grace made itself known in the form of Boaz. Law knows no mercy; it demands only justice. Grace, however, looks for a way to satisfy the law's demands and bring happiness and joy to the guilty. Like Ruth, we had no legal claim to God's blessings. However, because Christ, the heavenly Boaz, has removed the curse of sin and death from us we now joyfully live in His reflected glory. It comes to us from Him.

O Father, that I should receive any glory at all – even a reflected glory – is beyond my comprehension. All I can say is that the glory You give to me, I will give back to You. Amen.

Wedding in the skies

FOR READING AND MEDITATION
RUTH 4:13–17

'The women living there said, "Naomi has a son." And they named him Obed.' (v.17)

At this moment our Saviour is in heaven doing many things, but one in particular – He is attending to the arrangements for the wedding that is one day to take place between Himself and His Church. We, the bride of Christ here on earth, are expected to wait patiently for the day when He will come to receive us to Himself. Just as Ruth waited patiently to hear the voice of the maidens who, as was the custom, came to accompany the bride to her wedding, crying out 'Behold, the bridegroom cometh', so we too wait for that same cry that will herald the return of our Lord. We are going to a wedding in the skies which, by the way, is not called the wedding of the Church, but the wedding of the Lamb (Rev. 19:7).

Lord Jesus Christ, help me wait for Your coming down here on earth as You wait for it in heaven. I wait with patience – but also with eager anticipation. Amen.

From a mess – a message

FOR READING AND MEDITATION
RUTH 4:18–22

'Obed the father of Jesse, and Jesse the father of David.'
(v.22)

What is the book of Ruth saying to us? This – through all the mistakes, blunders, heartaches, problems and difficulties of life, God is continually at work, guiding, governing and controlling all our days. So learn to drop your anchor into the depths of this reassuring and encouraging revelation: out of every mess God is able to make a message. Never forget that the God and Father of Ruth, Boaz and Naomi, is also the God and Father of our Lord Jesus Christ, and through our Kinsman-Redeemer has become our God as well. In heaven He is preparing for us a new home where we will abide with Him for ever. Ruth reveals so much to us of the goodness and sovereignty of God that our lives cannot help but be enriched.

Father, thank You for showing me in such great detail the truth that You have the power and ability to turn a tragedy into a triumph. I rejoice in Jesus' name. Amen.

Living dangerously

FOR READING AND MEDITATION
ESTHER 4:10–17

'So Mordecai went away and carried out all of Esther's instructions.' (v.17)

The verse I have chosen is without doubt the highlight of the book and introduces us to its main message and theme – the sovereignty of God at work in the lives of His people. In a way, this theme is similar to Ruth, and I make no apology for exposing you yet again to this subject. Unless we hold in our hearts the solid conviction that God is on the throne, our lives will soon become drained of all point and purpose. The Christian who says, 'I am not sure whether God is at work in my life or not', is living dangerously. The way we think greatly influences the way we feel, and if our perception of things is that they are haphazard and without point and purpose then we will live unfulfilled lives.

Father, I realise that when I live out my days here on earth with no clear understanding of Your overall direction and control, I live dangerously. May I understand Your divine sovereignty. Amen.

A fixed point

FOR READING AND MEDITATION
ESTHER 7:1–10

'So they hanged Haman on the gallows he had prepared for Mordecai.' (v.10)

The second highlight of the book of Esther is the downfall and defeat of the scheming Haman. This verse, and the one we looked at yesterday, form the two hinges on which the book turns. One shows us the sovereignty of God in placing Esther in the king's palace during a time of impending peril, and the other points to the ultimate end of evil. We must hold in our hearts the solid conviction that God is on the throne, and no matter how things appear, it is His purposes that eventually hold sway. We are in a spiritual storm of satanic proportions. Just as a mariner takes his bearings from fixed points to steer safely through dangerous oceans, so we need the fixed points of God's Word to avoid spiritual shipwreck.

My Father and my God, I am on a difficult journey through life but I am thankful that You have charted my course with care and provided the fixed points of Your Word. Amen.

World Fair – 482 BC

FOR READING AND MEDITATION
ESTHER 1:1–8

'... in the third year of his reign he gave a banquet for all his nobles and officials.' (v.3)

E sther is one of the two books of the Old Testament on which an orthodox Jew is required to make any solemn oath or vow – the other being the Pentateuch, the books of Moses. The reason for this is that Moses recounts the deliverance of the Jews from Egypt, and the book of Esther recounts the deliverance of the Jews from what could have been one of the greatest massacres of all time. The opening verses of Esther introduce us to a sensual and capricious king called Xerxes (known in Hebrew as Ahasuerus). One day he decided to put on a great pageant for his lords and ladies – a kind of World Fair. The planning of this great celebration took six months and culminated with a magnificent banquet (v.5).

Gracious and loving Father, thank You for Your great deliverance. In Jesus' name. Amen.

Wifely submission

FOR READING AND MEDITATION
ESTHER 1:10–12

*'But when the attendants delivered the king's command,
Queen Vashti refused to come.' (v.12)*

Some commentators believe Xerxes wanted Vashti to
disrobe in front of his guests. This would explain why
she refused to obey the king's command. God does not
require a wife to submit to her husband when he wants
her to do something that goes against Scripture. But the
matter must not be left there. Any woman faced with
a command from her husband to do something wrong,
improper and unscriptural, ought to ask God for wisdom
to come up with a creative alternative. Remember what
Daniel did when asked to violate Scripture? He came
up with a creative alternative that went some way to
meeting the king's desires but did not compromise his
convictions (Dan. 1:8–16).

*Father, I see that although submission to authority is a
clear biblical principle, I am never expected to obey any
command that violates Your Word. Help me to be wise,
submissive and creative. Amen.*

Loving leadership

FOR READING AND MEDITATION
ESTHER 1:13–22

'... the queen's conduct will become known to all the women, and so they will despise their husbands ...' (v.17)

Some Christian husbands adopt a harsh attitude in their marriages. They say: 'I am the head and that means I must be obeyed at all costs. God has made this decree in His Word and I am here to enforce it.' It is perfectly true that God gives spiritual headship to the man in marriage, but that headship is to be operated under the law of love. A man is to love his wife and lead her as Christ loves the Church (Eph. 5:25). And how does Christ lead and love the Church? With great tenderness and sensitivity. Any husband who says, 'I'm the boss so you had better obey' is not following the leadership example of Christ. He is not a leader; he is a dictator. And such an attitude is alien to the Spirit of Christ.

Father, I know that it takes great skill to handle a relationship, especially that of marriage. Help me bring the attitude of Jesus into all my relationships. Amen.

Enter Mordecai

FOR READING AND MEDITATION
ESTHER 2:1–6

'Now there was in the citadel of Susa a Jew of the tribe of Benjamin.' (v.5)

The first 'Miss World' contest begins. At this point a third person appears in our story – Mordecai the Jew. Mordecai's great-grandfather had been taken into captivity in Babylon over 100 years before, in the days of Nebuchadnezzar, in company with such famous names as Daniel and Ezekiel. About 60 years before the events recorded in Esther, in 539 BC, Cyrus the Persian conquered Babylon. He issued a decree allowing the Jews to return to Jerusalem to rebuild the Temple. Many exiles returned to Jerusalem, but others preferred to stay in Babylon or move to other parts of the Persian empire. Mordecai settled in Susa, one of the Persian capitals. He was the right man in the right place at the right time.

O Father, forgive me that I am so slow to recognise Your guiding and governing hand in my life. Make me alert and sensitive to the fact that I am being guided, even when I am not aware of it. Amen.

'Beautiful and lovely'

FOR READING AND MEDITATION
ESTHER 2:7–8

'… the maiden was beautiful and lovely …' (v.7, RSV)

It is surely significant that we are introduced to Esther with these words: 'The maiden was beautiful and lovely'. Why significant? Because these words imply she was a woman fit to be a queen. Most Jews in that period of time regarded a mixed marriage as something to be strictly avoided. Yet Mordecai entered Esther in the contest. This is what we mean when we talk about the sovereignty of God. It makes itself known in many different ways, one being the gentle pressure that the Almighty places on a person's mind, urging him to do or say something that might be against his natural inclinations. And however difficult that is to understand, one discovers that God's leadings always turn out right.

O Father, where would I be today were it not for Your sovereign purposes quietly being worked out in my life? How grateful I am for the gentle pressure of Your Holy Spirit. Amen.

When plans are crossed

FOR READING AND MEDITATION
ESTHER 2:8–9

'The girl pleased him and won his favour.' (v.9)

One of the fascinating things about Old Testament history is the way God used those who did not believe in Him to further His purposes. Cyrus, the creator of the Persian empire, is one such example. Yet Isaiah shows us how, behind all his conquests, a divine purpose was at work: 'I will strengthen you though you have not acknowledged me' (Isa. 45:5). We discover a similar pattern in the passage before us today. We begin to see now even more clearly why Mordecai and Esther were in the royal city of Susa and had not returned to Jerusalem to help rebuild it. Remember, the next time your personal plans are overturned, God allows our own plans to be broken so that we, with Him, can build bigger and better ones.

Gracious and loving heavenly Father, may I ever be open to the possibility that in the thwarting of my plans, greater and wiser purposes are being worked out. Amen.

Why anti-Semitism?

FOR READING AND MEDITATION
ESTHER 2:10

*'Esther had not revealed her nationality ... because
Mordecai had forbidden her to do so.' (v.10)*

What accounts for anti-Semitism? The real reason, I
think, is quite simply because the Jews are God's
chosen people. Not His only people, but a people chosen
to display a special purpose. When unregenerate people
who carry within them a hatred of God meet those whom
God has marked out for a special purpose, they often
transfer the feelings of hatred they have towards God
to the people who represent Him. This, I believe, is the
major dynamic behind anti-Semitism. Also, it explains
why an anti-Semite who becomes a Christian finds that
his love for God flows over into a new-found love for the
Jews. Loving God, he loves in a special way all those who
are part of His eternal purposes.

*Father, how thrilling it is to note that since I have come to
know You, my love has expanded to take in others who
once were outside my circle. Amen.*

God's patience

FOR READING AND MEDITATION
ESTHER 2:11–14

'... a girl ... had to complete twelve months of beauty treatments ...' (v.12)

Mordecai's daily vigil at the palace gate went on not for a period of a few weeks, but for twelve months! Am I talking today to someone who has been waiting for a long time to learn the outcome of an issue on which important matters are resting? Does it seem at times that God has forgotten the promise He made and has abandoned you? Ah, this is a problem that has confronted many of God's people down the ages. It puzzled the psalmist and it perplexed most of the prophets. Why does God appear to be so slow and unhurried? Let me put it as plainly as I can – God does not work our way. His patience is something we can never truly grasp or comprehend. We must learn to have patience with the patience of God.

Heavenly Father, forgive me for my impatience with Your patience. Help me understand that with You things never get off course. You may seem slow, but You are always sure. Amen.

Chosen as queen

FOR READING AND MEDITATION
ESTHER 2:15–20

'Now the king was attracted to Esther more than to any of the other women ...' (v.17)

Esther is the new queen of the land without her Jewish identity being made known. Quietly and unhurriedly, God has brought about the first stage in His plans to protect and deliver His people. We must use this example to reinforce the conviction that ought to be in the heart of every Christian, namely the fact that God never vacates His throne. Let me assure you once again that even though there may be times when God appears to have no interest in the march of the moments, He is working out His purposes nevertheless. Only blind ignorance interprets His silence as weakness. As a poet once put it – history is His story!

O Father, drive this powerful and important truth more deeply into my spirit than it has ever been before. May it be an anchor that will hold me steady in the most fierce of storms. Amen.

A plot uncovered

FOR READING AND MEDITATION
ESTHER 2:21–23

'Mordecai found out about the plot and told Queen
Esther, who … reported it to the king …' (v.22)

Now that God has successfully brought Esther into
favour with the king, His purpose is to do exactly
the same for Mordecai. Isn't it amazing that an unknown
Jew such as Mordecai became a favoured subject of
the king? After the plotters were hanged, a record is
made of the whole episode, right down to the name of
Mordecai who had first informed about the matter. How
painstaking and precise is divine sovereignty! Every 'i' is
dotted and every 't' is crossed. Some see sovereignty as
concerned only with the steering of the stars but, believe
me, sometimes it has to do with such seemingly trivial
things as writing a letter, or catching a certain train. I say
again – nothing is too trivial for Omnipotence.

*Father, thank You that the tiniest details of my life are
important to You. I am grateful that You guide not only
the great and mighty planets but also the tiny movements
of my life. Amen.*

Stand tall!

FOR READING AND MEDITATION
ESTHER 3:1–4

'All the royal officials … knelt down … to Haman … But Mordecai would not kneel …' (v.2)

Mordecai was adamant – he would bow only to the Creator and not to a creature. Perhaps his friends argued that he ought to sacrifice principle for policy and thus live on to pursue his cause. Mordecai, however, refused to listen to the voice of expediency, believing it right to honour God no matter what the consequences. I have already warned you about the voice of expediency, and without hesitation I do so once again. Expediency can quickly ensnare the soul. It says: 'When in Rome do as the Romans do.' If there is ever a clash between principle and policy, stick to your principles. Let Mordecai's example rouse you to action. You may lose the world but you will save your soul.

Father, help me to remember that doing the right thing is always the right thing to do. Make me a person of principle so that my policies have something to keep them on course. Amen.

A diabolical plan

FOR READING AND MEDITATION
ESTHER 3:5–6

'Yet having learned who Mordecai's people were, he scorned the idea of killing only Mordecai.' (v.6)

Behind Haman's plans and ideas lies the arch-enemy of the human race himself – Satan. The devil knows there are two classes of people who are specially chosen by God in the world – the Jewish nation and the Church of God. And his hatred, as history shows, is aimed at both. If Satan had been able to exterminate the Jews then there would have been no Redeemer and no Saviour, for it was prophesied that our Lord would be of Jewish descent. The persecution of the Jews served, in turn, to keep them together and developed in them a strong and powerful desire to maintain their identity no matter what. Another evidence of how God uses adverse circumstances as 'grist to His mill'.

My Father and my God, the more I see how nothing can frustrate Your eternal purposes, the more I realise how unnecessary are my fears. Amen.

God's timepiece

FOR READING AND MEDITATION
ESTHER 3:7–8

'There is a certain people ... who keep themselves separate.' (v.8)

Right from the moment when Terah, the father of Abraham, and his family crossed the River Euphrates, and by so doing became the first people to be called 'Hebrews', meaning 'the people who crossed over', God has overshadowed them, guided them and protected them. Although far from perfect, the Jewish nation has been described as 'God's timepiece' because their movements accurately tell the world what time it is on God's clock of prophecy. Unless I am greatly mistaken, their return to the promised land in this, our own generation, and their strong national identity, mark a critical and important hour on God's clock of prophecy.

Father, can it be that I am passing through a vital hour in the history of the world and of humanity? Help me be alert and spiritually prepared for whatever is to happen. Amen.

A mismatched contest

FOR READING AND MEDITATION
ESTHER 3:9–15

'If it pleases the king, let a decree be issued to destroy them …' (v.9)

Haman's speech to the king was full of lies, which is not surprising when you consider that behind it was the one whom Jesus once referred to as 'the father of lies' – the devil (John 8:44). Once the decree was signed and sealed, it was translated into the many languages of the subject peoples and sent to every part of the empire. The edict said that on the 13th day of a certain month, every Jew would be put to death. No one would be exempt. It demanded complete extermination. Haman was to find out, however, what other leaders of nations throughout time have found – that those who set out to exterminate the Jews are fighting against God. And what a mismatched contest that always turns out to be!

Gracious and loving heavenly Father, how glad I am that I am not fighting against You, but You are fighting for me. Amen.

Always ahead!

FOR READING AND MEDITATION
ESTHER 4:1–9

'Hathach went back and reported to Esther what Mordecai had said.' (v.9)

Esther learns for the first time of Haman's plan to exterminate her people. Perhaps it was at this moment that Mordecai and Esther began to gain some insight into the purpose of their being in the royal city of Susa in Persia. Sometimes we fail to recognise the guidance of God until we are face to face with a crisis. Then how reassuring it is to know that the God who has foreseen everything, and has gone before us, is unfailingly at work to bring all things to a positive end. I was taught in Sunday school a song that went like this: 'He who has led, will lead.' Now, it is more than a song; it is a constant spiritual support.

O God, forgive me that I so easily forget You are not only around me, beneath me, and above me, but also ahead of me. Nothing can happen to me that You have not foreseen or anticipated. Amen.

More about sovereignty

FOR READING AND MEDITATION
ESTHER 4:10

'Then she instructed him to say to Mordecai ...' (v.10)

As Christians, we ought never to tire of talking about divine sovereignty. I know of no greater incentive to effective Christian living than to meditate on the fact that God is constantly at work in our lives, and that His guidance involves the tiniest details. A man I know puts his own assessment of the divine attention to detail in these words: 'If I had not met a certain person I would not have known a certain lady who introduced me to another person, and if that other person did not have a delicate daughter who was disturbed by the barking of my dog, I would not now be serving Christ in the way I am.' Who can deny that God orders the affairs of His children down to the tiniest details?

O Father, once again I stand in awe of Your marvellous attention to detail. You can use even the barking of a dog in the pursuit of Your eternal purposes. How wondrous are all Your ways. Amen.

'You have a destiny'

FOR READING AND MEDITATION
ESTHER 4:10–14

'And who knows but that you have come to royal position for such a time as this?' (v.14)

I believe that these words are the ones that God wants to come alive in your own life today. You too are a person of destiny, and have come into God's kingdom for such a time as this. A preacher tells how his young daughter came home from a Christian youth camp and said excitedly: 'Dad, they told me at camp I have a destiny.' Then about an hour or two later she said: 'Dad, what's a destiny?' She had one but didn't quite know what it was. Many Christians are like that. They are here for a purpose but they don't know what it is. God has destined you to do something particular, and if you don't do it, then it just won't get done. Part of my destiny is to write *Every Day with Jesus*. What's yours?

O Father, can it really be true that You have put me in Your kingdom to fulfil a purpose that is solely mine? I must believe it. Show me my destiny, dear Lord. Amen.

Time to fast

FOR READING AND MEDITATION
ESTHER 4:15-17

'Go, gather together all the Jews who are in Susa, and fast for me.' (v.15)

There are many reasons to fast but we need to beware hypocrisy (Isa. 58) and pride (Luke 18:9–14). It appears some situations require both prayer *and fasting* (Joel 1:14; 2:12–18). If you want to study the subject then I suggest you get hold of a good book on the matter, such as Arthur Wallis's *God's Chosen Fast*. I know of no better way when facing a crisis, or when about to make a major life decision, than to refrain from making any decisions until you have entered into a time of prayer and fasting. Even a 24-hour period of fasting can bring tremendous spiritual results. But one word of caution: no fasting should be done without medical counsel if there are any physical problems.

Father, are You trying to get my attention over this matter of fasting? Is this the voice of the Holy Spirit I hear? If so, help me be clear about the matter. Make me both willing and obedient. Amen.

The royal sceptre

FOR READING AND MEDITATION
ESTHER 5:1–2

'When he saw Queen Esther ... he ... held out to her the gold sceptre ...' (v.2)

Although Esther has fasted and prayed, this does not relieve her of the need to approach the king personally. Prayer and fasting sharpen our spiritual focus and enable us to take the right and most effective action. What a splendid picture this is of the way we sinners are accepted by the Almighty. God, we are told, has a 'sceptre of righteousness' (Heb. 1:8, AV), which represents His purity and holiness. We are not pure enough to approach Him ourselves. However, dressed in the robe of righteousness that Christ provides, we are able to come before God, touch the sceptre of His burning purity which He holds out to us, and be welcomed into the divine presence as if we had never sinned.

Father, how can I sufficiently thank You that because of the shed blood of the Lord Jesus Christ I don't need an invitation to come into Your presence? I can stand before You at any time. Amen.

The divine strategy

FOR READING AND MEDITATION
ESTHER 5:3–8

*'If it pleases the king … let the king, together with Haman,
come today to a banquet …' (v.4)*

Why this strange procedure of banquets? We are watching the wisdom of God at work, flowing through a human mind. As Esther waited before God in those three days of fasting, her thoughts were quietly taken over by God's thoughts. Her mind flowed into His mind and His mind flowed into her mind. How this illustrates the need to prayerfully soak our minds in the Word of God – daily. As I have told you many times before – human ingenuity and wisdom are utterly inadequate to meet the demands of daily living. If we are to live every day victoriously then we must spend more time with the Lord in prayer, and meditate on His Word. That is really the only place where we can exchange our thoughts for His.

O Father, forgive me for trying to battle against life in my own strength and with my own thoughts, when You are so willing to give me Your strength and Your thoughts. Amen.

Wrong counsel

FOR READING AND MEDITATION
ESTHER 5:9–14

'His wife Zeresh ... said ... "Have a gallows built ... and ask the king in the morning to have Mordecai hanged on it."' (v.14)

Haman's wife, Zeresh, suggests building a gallows to hang Mordecai. The power and influence that lies in the hands of a wife is tremendous – for good or evil. She has the ability to open a trap door through which her husband can fall to oblivion and despair, or erect a ladder by which he can climb to achievement and success. Blessed is the man with a good and godly wife who understands the power and influence that lies within her grasp and co-operates with the Almighty in making her husband the man God wants him to be.

Gracious and loving heavenly Father, thank You for the power and influence that lies within every relationship – especially that of marriage. Help us use that power in the right way. Amen.

A sleepless night!

FOR READING AND MEDITATION
ESTHER 6:1–3

'"What honour and recognition has Mordecai received for this?" the king asked.' (v.3)

The great King Xerxes, despite his comfortable bed and luxurious surroundings, is unable to sleep! It has nothing to do with the food he has eaten at the banquet. God is at work in his life to see he is kept awake. We ought never to forget that the Almighty can reach into a human heart at any time. Can you see what is happening here? The hand of destiny is at work and the stage is being set for the last few scenes in the drama of God versus Haman. I heard a preacher say: 'I feel sorry for anyone who tries to set out and involve himself in a programme that defiantly flies in the face of God.' So do I. God wins every argument, every battle and every cause. All the time!

O Father, the way Your power and wisdom combine to resolve problems is so awesome and astonishing. Help me come through to a greater trust in You. Amen.

Indestructible!

FOR READING AND MEDITATION
ESTHER 6:4–14

'Since Mordecai ... is of Jewish origin ... you will surely come to ruin!' (v.13)

Can you imagine Haman's feelings as, in obedience to the king's command, he has to go to Mordecai, assist him to mount the king's horse and then lead him through the city, calling on all to respect the man whom the king has decided to honour? Shamed and humiliated, Haman returns to his home, morally and politically defeated. There his advisers pronounce the significant words of our text for today. These are indeed solemn and powerful words, and they have as much force today as they did then. Those who seek to completely destroy the people called the Jews must first destroy God.

Father, this is not only true of the Jews, it is also true of the Church. To destroy me the devil would first have to destroy You. This means I am undefeatable and indestructible. Amen.

The groan of God

FOR READING AND MEDITATION
ESTHER 7:1–4

'If it pleases your majesty, grant me my life … And spare my people …' (v.3)

Esther's intercession is a model that all Christians would do well to emulate. She is bold, plain, simple and direct. She identifies herself with the Jewish people and humbly pleads for their deliverance. All intercession begins in identification. It starts when we allow the groan of God to develop in our souls. How were the slaves freed in the British empire? One man, by the name of William Wilberforce, set out with the groan of God in his soul and laboured fervently until the slaves were freed. How did my own nation of Wales receive a divine visitation in 1904? God groaned in the heart of a man named Evan Roberts and he prayed through until victory came and revival swept through the land.

O God, I open my soul afresh to You today and invite You to groan in me. Whatever concern You feel, I must share with You. Place it upon my heart, dear Lord. Amen.

The tables are turned

FOR READING AND MEDITATION
ESTHER 7:3–10

*'So they hanged Haman on the gallows he had prepared
for Mordecai.' (v.10)*

This is a rather terrifying story, but who can feel sorry
that Haman had the tables turned on him? He died
that day on the very gallows that he had constructed for
Mordecai. Let this thought enter your soul right now,
and carry it with you through the rest of your days on
earth – God may permit the devil to push us right to the
edge of disaster, but He will not allow him to push us
over. When we are linked to God and His purposes then
we may have some very frightening and scary moments,
but these ought only to intensify our intercessions and
deepen our dependency and trust in the Christ-linked life.
Everything that happens works towards divine ends.

*O Father, I am so thankful for the way the truths of Your
Word feed my spirit. Nothing is purposeless and nothing
can work against You. Blessed be Your wonderful name.
Amen.*

The 'undefeatable' God

FOR READING AND MEDITATION
ESTHER 8:1–2

'The king took off his signet ring … reclaimed from Haman, and presented it to Mordecai.'(v.2)

God's plans are undefeatable because of His foreknowledge. Because He sees everything that is going to happen in the future, He is able to outmanoeuvre whatever may be contrary to His purposes. Satan does not possess foreknowledge. This is quite clear from the events that took place at the cross. Satan thought he had brought Christ down into death, but found that the very thing he planned would defeat Christ – the cross – actually contributed to His greatest victory. What does all this say to us? It says you can go out into the day knowing that God has foreseen every trick that the devil may use upon you, and outwit and outmanoeuvre him in a way that will enrich your life and bring glory to Christ's name.

Father, I am consoled by the thought that You and You alone know the end from the beginning. Though Satan is obviously a being of great power and ability, he is clearly no match for You. Amen.

The good news

FOR READING AND MEDITATION
ESTHER 8:3-17

'Now write another decree in the king's name on behalf of the Jews ...' (v.8)

How wonderfully these events illustrate the story of the gospel of our Lord Jesus Christ. God's law of holiness, just like the laws of the Medes and Persians, is inviolable. The scripture declares clearly and emphatically: 'The soul who sins is the one who will die' (Ezek. 18:4). Nothing could be done to revoke that edict. Christ, however, by His intervention on the cross, took our sins into Himself and thereby brought into existence a new law that ensures that all who come and stand at the cross and accept Him as their Lord and Saviour will be saved. That new law, too, has been published in many languages and carried to the farthest parts of the earth. It is called, as you know, 'the good news'.

Father, how marvellous is the message of the gospel. Your law demanded my death, but Your love arranged for Jesus to die in my place. Help me to be a faithful messenger of this new 'law'. Amen.

A special memorial

FOR READING AND MEDITATION
ESTHER 9:1–22

'Mordecai ... sent letters to all the Jews ... to have them celebrate annually ...' (vv.20–21)

Following this great day of deliverance, Mordecai makes moves to establish it as an annual memorial throughout all generations. Now, some 2,500 years later, Jews celebrate the event every year in a feast that they call the Feast of Purim. Christians have a special memorial too. It is called the 'table of communion', a simple but meaningful ceremony that God has established in the Church to remind us of that glorious day at Calvary when Satan's plans were wrecked, and salvation was made available to all humanity. May that memorial become more meaningful to us every time we participate in it.

O Father, Your deliverance for me on the cross is a spiritual deliverance, not merely a physical one. May the wonder of it sink deeper and deeper within me. In Jesus' name I pray. Amen.

Victory every day

FOR READING AND MEDITATION
ESTHER 9:23; 10:3

'Mordecai the Jew was second in rank to King Xerxes ...'
(10:3)

The Jews, in looking back over their history, give thanks to God for those occasions when He worked in great power to effect their deliverance, by setting aside special dates and seasons. But such is the breathtaking wonder of God's grace to believers that really there are just not enough days to go round. When, after World War II, Europe celebrated victory over the Nazis, they called it VE Day – Victory in Europe. Some years later, a boy was asked by his history teacher what VE Day stood for. He replied: 'Victory Every Day'. In the light of God's sovereignty and love, we who are His redeemed children can live out our lives in full assurance of certain victory – this day and every day. Our God reigns!

Father, let my consciousness be filled with the thought that the same loving sovereignty and care that went into the planning of Ruth's and Esther's lives is also at work in mine. Amen.

Hard sayings!

FOR READING AND MEDITATION
MATTHEW 13:47–58

'"Where then did this man get all these things?" And they took offence at him.' (vv.56–57)

Why is it that so many churches proclaim only half the gospel – the attractive half? It is true that our Lord is risen from the dead and offers peace, joy and the promise of heaven to those who believe, but there is another side to the gospel. I refer to some of our Lord's sayings such as dying in order to live, losing in order to find, going down in order to go up, success through failure, and so on. When we ignore what have been called 'the hard sayings of Jesus', we end up with a form of Christianity that has little cutting edge and is devoid of power. Focusing only on the attractive part of the gospel may fill the pews, but it leaves the heart half empty. Remember, 'it is only as we grapple that we grow'.

O God, You know the biting hesitation that fills my heart when I sense You are calling me to higher things. Yet I realise it is only as I am challenged that I change. Amen.

Does Jesus offend you?

FOR READING AND MEDITATION
LUKE 7:18–28

'Blessed is the man who does not fall away on account of me.' (v.23)

The hard sayings of Jesus contain thoughts and ideas that challenge our self-centredness and cut deep into our carnal nature. Sometimes our Lord's principles appear downright offensive. For example: 'Follow me, and let the dead bury their own dead' (Matt. 8:22). Or this statement made to the Syro-Phoenician woman: 'Let the children eat all they want … for it is not right to take the children's bread and toss it to their dogs' (Mark 7:27). These hard sayings of Jesus (and there are many more) present us with tough issues that we have to wrestle with in order to fully comprehend them. If we refuse to face these issues then, although we may call ourselves Christians, we cannot really call ourselves disciples.

Father, help me see that as Your ways and thoughts are so different from mine, Your truth sometimes seems hard and offensive to my carnal nature. Help me see that it is I who am in the wrong. Amen.

'There is a cure'

FOR READING AND MEDITATION
ROMANS 9:22–33

'See, I lay in Zion a stone that causes men to stumble …'
(v.33)

There are times when Christ's words do more than just offend – they shock. For example: '… because you are lukewarm … I am about to spit you out of my mouth' (Rev. 3:16). He loves us too much not to confront us whenever we need it for He knows that when confrontation is necessary, not to confront is a failure in love. He is like a doctor who takes an X-ray and faces the patient with bad news. The patient is discomforted for a few moments until the doctor smiles and says: 'But there is a cure.' Our Lord loves us too much to let us get away with things that hinder our spiritual growth and maturity. He challenges us not simply to upset us, but to set us up.

O Lord, the challenges of Your Word sometimes cause my inner being to tremble. But help me realise that it is those very tremblings that shake me from self-sufficiency to Christ-sufficiency. Amen.

Jesus, the *Scandalon*

FOR READING AND MEDITATION
I PETER 2:1–12

'A stone that causes men to stumble and a rock that makes them fall.' (v.8)

In the passage before us today our Lord is referred to as 'a stone that causes men to stumble'. The Greek word for stumbling stone is *scandalon*, from which we get the word 'scandalised'. In its verb form it means 'to be offended'. The more we study the life of our Lord, the more we see how the things He said caused many people to be offended by Him. The laws of His kingdom didn't mesh with the dominant cultural trends of the day, and those who were secure and entrenched in their self-centred lifestyle, and wished to remain so, rose up in opposition to Him. Even some of His disciples were occasionally offended by Him. We prefer the 'soft' sayings of Jesus to His 'hard' sayings but we need to study both.

Father, I see that I have been brought into an upside-down kingdom, the values of which run counter to the way of the world. Help me grasp this fact so that I might work to turn things the right way up. Amen.

A trail of offence

FOR READING AND MEDITATION
MATTHEW 15:1–20

'... the disciples ... asked, "Do you know that the
Pharisees were offended when they heard this?"' (v.12)

Jesus began to offend before He was even born. What
could be more offensive than a fiancée who turns up
pregnant? During His ministry He left behind a trail of
offended people. The priests were offended by Him; not
only did He usurp their authority by overturning the
tables of those using the Temple as a marketplace, but
He talked about offering Himself as a perfect sacrifice.
The Pharisees were deeply incensed by Him when He
pronounced on them a list of terrible woes (Luke 11:42–
52). On one occasion even those who were close to Him,
members of His own family, appeared to be offended by
Him saying: 'He is out of his mind' (Mark 3:21). Can
anyone get close to Jesus without in some way being
offended by Him?

*Father, forgive me for not seeing that when Your words
offend me it is because I am more interested in myself than
I am in You. Don't stop pruning me, my Father. Amen.*

The Baptist's dilemma

FOR READING AND MEDITATION
MATTHEW 11:1–19

'Among those born of women there has not risen anyone greater than John the Baptist ...' (v.11)

Even John the Baptist stumbled because of Jesus. When he was put in prison, he sent his disciples to Jesus to ask the staggering question: 'Are you the one who was to come, or should we expect someone else?' Jesus' reply to John was this: 'Blessed is he who takes no *offence* at me' (v.6, RSV). On several occasions Jesus' own disciples stumbled because of Him. When Jesus spoke of eating His flesh and drinking His blood, many of His disciples grumbled and said: 'This is a hard teaching. Who can accept it?' 'Does this offend you?' Jesus asked. John writes that many turned back and no longer followed Him but Peter recognised that the words of eternal life are worth being offended for (John 6:60–69).

Father, help me have the attitude of Simon Peter who saw that the words of eternal life were worth being offended for. Move me on, dear Father, towards radical and wholehearted discipleship. Amen.

The good news is …

FOR READING AND MEDITATION
MATTHEW 21:33–46

'He who falls on this stone will be broken to pieces, but he on whom it falls will be crushed.' (v.44)

One preacher said: 'The gospel contains "good" news and "bad" news.' He went on to explain that there are attractive parts and unattractive parts. But he failed to explain that there are reasons for those unattractive parts of the gospel – they challenge us to deeper discipleship. I have a difficulty with those Christians who refer to the hard sayings of Jesus as 'bad news'. I just wish they would go on to explain that the good news is that the bad news is good. If we fall on Him we will be broken to pieces; if we don't fall on Him then we will be crushed. Either way we are going to get broken but if we stumble because of Christ and are broken, then we can be made truly whole – and that is good news.

Father, the severity of Your Word sometimes shakes me – even shocks me. But You hurt me in order to heal me. Help me ever to remember that. In Jesus' name. Amen.

A cause of 'deafness'

FOR READING AND MEDITATION
JOHN 6:51-69

*'I am the living bread … If a man eats of this bread, he
will live for ever.' (v.51)*

F.F. Bruce says: 'The implication [of verse 60] is that
they not only found it difficult to understand, but
suspected that, if they did understand it, they would
find it unacceptable.' One of the major reasons why so
many say they struggle with the words of Jesus is they
don't want to understand, because deep down in their
hearts they sense that if they did understand, they might
open themselves up to a challenge they would rather not
receive. Remember the old saying: 'There are none so deaf
as those who do not wish to hear'? This is why the Spirit
prefaced His remarks to the seven churches of Asia with
the words: 'Blessed are those who hear [this prophecy]
and take to heart what is written in it' (Rev. 1:3).

*Father, can it be that the reason I often don't understand is
because I don't want to understand? Forgive me and help
me have an open ear and an open heart. Amen.*

Winning – yet winnowing

FOR READING AND MEDITATION
JOHN 6:25–51

'But there is the bread that comes down from heaven,
which a man may eat and not die.' (v.50)

To understand what Jesus was saying here we have to set His words against the backdrop of the miracle of the feeding of the multitude. There is no doubt that our Lord's popularity following this miracle was very high but, as Dr Campbell Morgan points out: 'Christ was not only winning but also winnowing.' Once their stomachs were full, He began to get to grips with the deeper issues of life – the spiritual issues. He says in effect: 'Not only can I give you the natural bread of life; I can also give you the spiritual bread of life. In fact, I am the Bread of Life. Eat of Me.' But the idea repelled them. They stumbled because of Him and that left just one alternative – eventually they would be crushed by Him.

O Father, I see that to stumble because of Your words
and not to respond by faith means that those very words
become not my redemption but my ruin. Lord, increase my
faith. Amen.

The Lord of miracles

FOR READING AND MEDITATION
LUKE 17:1–19

'Jesus asked, "Were not all ten cleansed? Where are the other nine?"' (v.17)

Jesus drew people to Himself by meeting their physical needs and then challenged them concerning their spiritual needs. What they stumbled over, then, is what multitudes stumble over today – more is required than just hearing the words of Jesus, we must be united with Him by faith, we must let our lives flow into Him and His life flow into us. Isn't it sad that people are ready to receive any kind of miracle from the hands of Christ except the miracle of eternal life? In my time I have known hundreds for whom the Lord has worked tremendous miracles, but when faced with the issue of surrendering their lives to Him, they drew back in fear. People want the miracles of the Lord, but not the Lord of miracles.

Father, my heart overflows with gratitude for the many miracles You have wrought in my life, but I want to thank You now for the greatest miracle of them all – my eternal salvation. Amen.

Feed on Him

FOR READING AND MEDITATION
MATTHEW 26:17–30

'This is my blood of the covenant, which is poured out for many for the forgiveness of sins.' (v.28)

What could Jesus have really meant when He talked about eating His flesh and drinking His blood? Jesus responded to the protest His words aroused by saying that they were not to be understood literally, but spiritually: 'The Spirit gives life; the flesh counts for nothing. The words I have spoken to you are spirit and they are life' (John 6:63). The truth is summed up most beautifully in the *Book of Common Prayer*: 'Take and eat this in remembrance that Christ died for thee, and feed on Him in thy heart by faith with thanksgiving.' To feed on Christ in one's heart by faith with thanksgiving is to eat His flesh, drink His blood, and so have eternal life.

My Saviour and my God, help me to feed on You, not only at the time when I take Communion, but every waking minute of every hour and of every day. Amen.

One hundred per cent!

FOR READING AND MEDITATION
PHILIPPIANS 3:1-14

'I want to know Christ ... becoming like him in his death ...' (v.10)

Most of these hard sayings of Jesus are challenges to deeper discipleship. Our Lord is saying in effect: 'I am not interested in being just a figure in a holy book or subject of theological discussion. I want you to be so taken up with Me, so absorbed by Me, so indwelt by Me, so captivated by Me, that you will be willing to die for Me. I want there to be no rival in your life. I want your life to be intertwined with Mine. I want you to be drenched by My love, saturated by My energy, and live in such a close relationship with Me that nothing shall ever be able to pull us apart.' If we are not prepared to commit ourselves one hundred per cent to Christ then we have no right to call ourselves His disciples.

Father, hold me steady as I face these burning issues. Let there be no dodging, no turning, no excuses. Keep me true to You in everything and make me a one hundred per cent disciple. Amen.

Can this be true?

FOR READING AND MEDITATION
LUKE 14:25–33

'…. any of you who does not give up everything he has cannot be my disciple.' (v.33)

Another of the hard sayings of Jesus is: 'If anyone comes to me and does not hate his father and mother, his wife and children, his brothers and sisters – yes, even his own life – he cannot be my disciple' (v.26). What can Jesus mean when He asks us to hate our families? Our Lord is concerned that His disciples allow nothing to come between Him and them – particularly family ties. The interests of God's kingdom must be paramount with the followers of Jesus. Everything must take second place to them, even love for one's family. No wonder critics of Christianity see this statement and attitude of Jesus as scandalous. Does it shock you? Good. That is exactly what it is designed to do.

Lord Jesus Christ, my Saviour and my God, I know You well enough to realise that behind all Your statements is a heart of love. Help me believe in You even when I cannot understand You. Amen.

Drawing blood

FOR READING AND MEDITATION
MARK 7:1–13

'Thus you nullify the word of God by your tradition that you have handed down.' (v.13)

Jesus censured those theologians who argued that people who had vowed to give God a sum of money, were not then free to use that money in order to meet their parents' pressing need. Jesus quite clearly disagrees with this and states categorically that not to give the money to their parents would be a violation of the commandment to honour one's father and mother. How can this be reconciled with 'hating' our families? Jesus uses these hard sayings that seem to run contrary to His general teaching to test the spiritual mettle of those who profess to be interested in Him and His cause. Sometimes our Lord's sayings are so sharp they metaphorically draw blood. Many then reject Him and involve themselves no further.

Father, help me be a disciple who is honest enough to admit to confusion at some of the things You confront me with, but determined enough to go through with You at any cost. Amen.

Intentionally shocking

FOR READING AND MEDITATION
I TIMOTHY 5:1–25

'If anyone does not provide for his relatives ... he has denied the faith ... ' (v.8)

However we look at it, hating one's relatives is a shocking idea. But then, from our Lord's point of view, *it was meant to be shocking.* Although our Lord commends those who have a deep concern and interest in their families, He is against them being so preoccupied with family matters and interests that they have no time for the interests of the kingdom of God. Jesus strongly deprecates the inward-looking attitude that puts self and personal interests at the centre, and sometimes the only way one can see this evil is to be shocked into seeing it. Love of self can dress up in the smartest of clothes, but such a suit or costume is not the right apparel for a disciple. Hence it must be exposed.

Father, help me understand how I can provide for and love my relatives without them replacing You as the centre of my affections. In Jesus' name. Amen.

'Hate' scrutinised

FOR READING AND MEDITATION
DEUTERONOMY 21:10–21

'If a man has two wives, one beloved, and another hated, and they have born him children … ' (v.15, AV)

The purpose behind today's passage is to prevent a man from showing favouritism when he allocates his property to his heirs. *In the biblical idiom the term 'hate' means to love less.* On another occasion Jesus again presents the truth of the past few days, but in a less shocking way, when He says: 'Anyone who loves his father or mother more than me is not worthy of me; anyone who loves his son or daughter more than me is not worthy of me' (Matt.10:37). Our Lord is not against us loving our families; what He is against is us loving our families more than we love Him. He demands first place in our lives, and who can deny that what He demands is only what He deserves?

Father, I see that if I do not crown You Lord of all, I do not crown You Lord at all. Help me search my heart today to make sure that no one but You sits on the throne of my life. Amen.

'Nearest and dearest'

FOR READING AND MEDITATION
PSALM 73:1–28

'Whom have I in heaven but you? And being with you, I desire nothing on earth.' (v.25)

The declaration to 'hate' our families looked contradictory to Christ's other teachings. But our Lord never contradicted Himself. He did use paradoxes, but a paradox is quite different from a contradiction. His point then, and now, is that it is natural for people to care for their nearest and dearest. His disciples, though, must make Him the nearest and dearest. Jesus knew full well the natural resistance He would encounter in explaining true discipleship. So He made His point in the most surprising, arresting and challenging language at His command. The comforting Christ can also be the shocking Christ. But His shocks are never just for effect; they are meant to challenge and change.

Lord Jesus Christ, help me realise that when I have a pure love for You then I have the right kind of love to give to others. Bring me to that place – even though it means deeper challenges. Amen.

Jesus – violent?

FOR READING AND MEDITATION
MATTHEW 11:1–19

'The kingdom of heaven suffers violence, and the violent take it by force.' (v.12, NKJV)

The third of the hard sayings of Jesus is: 'The kingdom of heaven suffers violence, and the violent take it by force'. Once again we hit a problem – what Jesus is saying here seems to run counter to His general teaching on this subject. Christ clearly rejected brute force and violence as the means of advancement. In His general teaching He gives the impression that the heroes of the upside-down kingdom are not warrior kings riding in chariots, or peasants carrying pitchforks, but those who pursue their goals non-violently. He talks about humility, about kindness, about being like children, and about being servants. What, then, can He mean when He talks about taking the kingdom violently, by force?

Lord, again I come to something that on the face of it seems shocking and surprising. But knowing Your character helps me remain trustful whenever I am confused by the things You say or do. Amen.

Jesus the Revolutionary

FOR READING AND MEDITATION
LUKE 16:1–18

'... *the good news of the kingdom of God is being preached, and everyone is forcing his way into it.*' (v.16)

The Gospels show quite clearly that Jesus defied the ruling religious, political and economic powers but without violence. However, His clear teaching that the law of love superseded the dictates of human institutions certainly put Him in the category of a revolutionary. Purging the Temple of money-changers wasn't a mandate for violence either. It was a strong but measured response to the profiteering that was going on, and a reminder of what the Temple was all about. We have to admit that our Lord was a revolutionary, but the revolution He advanced was an upside-down revolution that replaced force with suffering, and violence with assertive love.

Lord Jesus, You who walked through an upside-down world with a message and a passion that was designed to turn it the right way up, give me something of that passion too. Amen.

The new Torah

FOR READING AND MEDITATION
JOHN 13:18–38

'A new commandment I give you: Love one another.'
(v.34)

The paramount example of Christ's non-violent attitude is the way He handled His death on the cross. Though violated, He refused to retaliate. With nails searing His flesh, He chose not to hate. Instead, He asked forgiveness for those who crucified Him, and in words that appeared to stretch the truth cried: 'Father, forgive them, for they do not know what they are doing' (Luke 23:34). His primary passion was the inauguration of a new kingdom – one that would grapple with poverty in an original way and without violence. Strange, then, that He should advocate taking the kingdom of heaven by violence and force?

Father, day by day I am seeing what discipleship really involves. It means trusting Your character, though doubts and uncertainties may arise. Help me to pass the tests of discipleship. Amen.

A volcanic eruption

FOR READING AND MEDITATION
LUKE 10:1–24

'I saw Satan fall like lightning from heaven.' (v.18)

The words of Jesus have to be seen in the context of this statement: *'And from the days of John the Baptist until now* the kingdom of heaven suffers violence' (Matt. 11:12, NKJV). Since the ministry of John had ended, the kingdom of heaven was on the march in a way that had never been seen before. Devils were being cast out (something the old age had been powerless to do), and in the kingdom of Satan a beachhead was being established with the force of a volcanic eruption. Clearly, Jesus was using the word 'violence' in the sense of forcefulness and aggressiveness. He was saying in effect: 'Since John the Baptist, the kingdom has been advancing in a way it has never advanced before.'

O Master, I know when I am following You I am following an aggressive Lover. You are going to establish Your kingdom, and no power in the universe can stop You. Amen.

No going back

FOR READING AND MEDITATION
LUKE 9:51–62

'No one who … looks back is fit for service in the kingdom of God.' (v.62)

Today we look at the second part of Christ's statement: 'and the violent take it by force'. What our Lord is saying here is this – because the kingdom of God is a kingdom that advances by spiritual forcefulness, then it follows that those who enter the kingdom and contribute to its advance must also have spiritual forcefulness – they must be men and women with courage, vigour and determination. In this hard saying, therefore, Jesus is putting the issue as clearly as He can – discipleship demands determination, courage, conviction and 'stickability'. Now, as then, it calls for courage and determination to be a disciple of God. The agenda of God's kingdom contains issues that only the truly committed can handle.

O Saviour, with the undaunted and determined faith, give me Your quiet confidence and resolve. Stamp these qualities deep within me so that I might follow You anywhere and everywhere. Amen.

The meaning of greatness

FOR READING AND MEDITATION
JOHN 13:1–17

'... *he poured water into a basin and began to wash his disciples' feet ...' (v.5)*

Now we examine another hard saying of Jesus: 'No servant is greater than his master, nor is a messenger greater than the one who sent him' (v.16). As the disciples sit around the table at the Last Supper another argument about greatness breaks out. In the midst of a sacred event, the disciples bicker about who should be first (Luke 22:24–27). Jesus lays aside His garments, takes a towel and a basin, and starts to wash the disciples' feet. We can only imagine the effect on the disciples as, in the midst of their power play, Jesus proceeds to wash their feet. He hoists the flag of His upside-down kingdom, picks up the tools of service, and says in effect: 'Greatness is found in serving, not in being served.'

Father, I see that in Your kingdom the way up is the way down. Oh, how desperately we, Your people, need to learn this lesson. Make this truth still more clear to us, even though it may hurt. Amen.

Tools of our trade

FOR READING AND MEDITATION
PHILIPPIANS 2:1–18

'Your attitude should be the same as that of Christ Jesus.'
(v.5)

Tools, we are told, define a trade. The basin and towel are the instruments of service, the tools of a servant. In ancient Israel they were usually never seen in the hands of masters, but in the hands of servants or slaves. These tools demand that a person takes a lower position and looks up rather than down. In this simple act, Jesus turned the old social hierarchies upside down and replaced them with a new one, namely, as we saw yesterday, one where greatness is found in serving, not in being served. As we become servants and wash each other's feet, the distinction between master and servant ends. Serving each other, we all simultaneously become the greatest in the kingdom.

O Father, if it is true that the basin and towel are the 'tools of my trade', then I confess my workmanship leaves much to be desired. Teach me how to serve others better. Amen.

Who is the greater?

FOR READING AND MEDITATION
JAMES 1:19–27

'… the man who looks intently into the perfect law that gives freedom … he will be blessed …' (v.25)

The lesson Jesus tried to teach the disciples – that greatness lies in serving and not in being served – is one of the hardest to learn. His words and actions as He stooped to wash the disciples' feet run counter to all our social customs and strike at the roots of fallen human nature. Waiters and waitresses are, as our American friends put it, a dime a dozen. Not in my kingdom, says Jesus. '… the greatest among you should be like the youngest, and the one who rules like the one who serves … I am among you as one who serves' (Luke 22:26–27). Of course, it must be made clear that our Lord is not asking that we turn our backs on earthly promotion. He is simply saying that is not where greatness lies.

Lord Jesus Christ, give me Your mind and attitudes on all matters. You pursue things vigorously, yet You are meek and lowly in heart. And I would be like You. Help me. Amen.

The Jesus way

FOR READING AND MEDITATION
MATTHEW 20:17–28

'... the Son of Man did not come to be served, but to serve ...' (v.28)

Jesus redefines greatness for us by telling us that it is an attitude – the attitude that concerns itself not with being served but with serving others. 'I am among you as one who serves,' He said (Luke 22:27). Instead of taking His place at the top of the hierarchy and looking down, seeing how many can serve Him, Jesus is at the bottom, looking up, and asking how many He can serve. Such an attitude flies in the face of modern-day individualism which emphasises the rights of the individual. Jesus calls us to humble servanthood, not assertive individualism. The Jesus style of service brought no financial gain, nor social prestige. We have just got to come to terms with this if we want to walk the Jesus way.

O Father, I want with all my heart to walk the Jesus way. But there is something within me that prefers to be served rather than to serve others, I ask now that You will root this out of me. Amen.

Improving your service

FOR READING AND MEDITATION
LUKE 14:7–14

'... *everyone who exalts himself will be humbled, and he who humbles himself will be exalted.*' (v.11)

Jesus, however, calls us to downward mobility. He asks us to take our seats at the bottom of the table. He asks us to draw from Him our status and significance and depend on Him for the strength we need to meet the challenges of every day. Those who are His true disciples happily defer to others and willingly yield up the good seats. In fact, the disciples of Jesus are so busy waiting on others they hardly have time to sit. Serving, not struggling for the best seat, is their main occupation. Those who exalt themselves will have to be content with a back seat in the kingdom. In this upside-down kingdom of Jesus, success depends, as in tennis, on how well you can serve.

O God, strengthen me with the Spirit of Jesus so that I may be prepared to adopt the way of serving as my way, whether others take it or not. I sit at the feet of the One who washes my feet! Amen.

Cross-bearing

FOR READING AND MEDITATION
LUKE 9:18–27

'What good is it for a man to gain the whole world, and yet lose or forfeit his very self?' (v.25)

The fifth hard saying of Jesus is about taking up our cross daily. This is perhaps one of the toughest tests a disciple can face for it involves self-denial, self-giving and self-effacement. The cross on which Jesus died was something He could not and would not avoid. God put it on Him. The cross spoken of in this saying, however, is something we can avoid – that is why we are challenged to take it up daily. Tragedies, accidents, sicknesses and misfortunes are not crosses in the sense in which the word is being used here. A cross, I remind you, is not something we are unable to avoid, but something we face and pick up. Be warned – cross-bearing is expensive and may have some costly consequences.

O Jesus, I am Your follower, yet the more I see Your demands, the more afraid I become. But I know Your way is right and I will take Your way, no matter what. Amen.

The self

FOR READING AND MEDITATION
MARK 8:27–38

'If anyone would come after me, he must deny himself and take up his cross and follow me.' (v.34)

What are some of the consequences of following Jesus with regard to the self? Well, first we are told to deny ourselves. But what does it mean, to deny ourselves? How do we understand this confusing matter of self? Is there any difference between self-denial and denial of self? The school of self-realisation – a typically Western position – says all the answers are in you. The school of self-renunciation – a typically Eastern position – says the self is a cancer and has to be cut out. One leaves you centred on yourself, the other leaves you with no self at all. To have a wrong idea about self will produce a wrong self, and a wrong self may mean a misspent life.

Father, I come to You asking that You wash my eyes and my heart. I want to see straight – especially on this issue of the self. Unfold it to me that I might see it from Your point of view. Amen.

Selfism

FOR READING AND MEDITATION
MATTHEW 18:1–5

'... whoever humbles himself like this child is the greatest
in the kingdom of heaven.' (v.4)

Eastern religions advocate getting rid of the self – self-
renunciation – but it is never actually eradicated.
Ultimately it rises up when provoked or offended. The
West adopts these three positions: know yourself, accept
yourself, express yourself. Just as I reject the Eastern view,
so I reject these popular Western views. Why? Because
they are attempts to deal with the self apart from God.
And any attempt to deal with the self outside of God
succeeds only in feeding the disease that it needs to cure
– self-centredness. Self in our own hands is a problem.
Self in God's hands is a power.

O God, this disease of selfism runs rampant in human
nature. Sin is its cause, but You are its cure. Teach me how
to be less self-centred and more Christ-centred. Amen.

Self-surrender

FOR READING AND MEDITATION
MATTHEW 6:25–34

'But seek first his kingdom and his righteousness, and all these things will be given to you as well.' (v.33)

The West adopts three main positions in relation to the self. Take the first: *Know yourself.* You can only know yourself in relation to the One who created you. Leave Him out of the picture and there is just no way you can really know yourself. *Accept yourself.* How can you accept a self that has at its roots a sinful condition? *Express yourself.* But if you have a crowd of people who have all been taught to express themselves – what have you got? You have a stage set for clash and confusion, jealousy and strife. The Christian answer is the surrender of yourself. This means getting yourself off your hands and into the hands of God. That's the safest place for the self I know.

God my Father, I see there is only one way to deal with self and that is to surrender it into Your hands. Teach me how to do this not merely on occasions but as a continual life practice. Amen.

Christo-centric

FOR READING AND MEDITATION
GALATIANS 2:11–21

'I have been crucified with Christ and I no longer live, but Christ lives in me.' (v.20)

If we think of the word 'ego' as a synonym for 'self' then we won't go far wrong. God wants us to move through life not as ego-centred people but as Christ-centred people. He is to be the centre and the ego is to revolve around Him. Any departure from this is a violation of the divine design. To deny ourselves, then, is to take the ego with all its desires and demands and surrender it to the interests of God's kingdom. Note I say 'self-surrender', not self-commitment. You may be committed to someone without being surrendered to him or her. A hard demand? Of course it is. This is why there are so few true disciples. As I understand it, discipleship involves nothing less and nothing more than self-surrender.

Father, I am deeply grateful for all Your confrontations for without them where would I be? You confront me in order to conquer me. My ego is Yours — Yours to command; mine to obey. Amen.

Is self cancelled?

FOR READING AND MEDITATION
PHILIPPIANS 1:12–26

'For to me, to live is Christ and to die is gain.' (v.21)

What happens to the self when it is surrendered to God? Some think it is completely wiped out, cancelled for all intents and purposes. But is this really true? Is self-surrender the kind of surgery to the soul that a lobotomy is to the brain? I do not believe so. When the self is surrendered to God He takes it and wipes it clean of self-interest and self-concern and, having cleansed us from selfishness, He gives it back to us. Lose yourself in God by self-surrender and you will find yourself. When you are His you are never more truly your own. It is the same kind of surrender that a loose wire makes when it surrenders itself to the dynamo. Now it throbs with energy, light and power.

Father, I see that when my will and Yours coincide then Your energy and my energy coincide also. I do everything for Your sake and by Your power. Amen.

Our own funeral

FOR READING AND MEDITATION
ROMANS 6:1–23

'... we know that our old self was crucified with him so
that ... we should no longer be slaves to sin ...' (v.6)

The way to life is through death. That death, however,
is death to the false life we have been living and to
the false ego that has been built up. The false, unnatural
world of sin and evil, the false self, organised around
egoism, has to die. We can never live in Christ, that
is really live, until we are prepared to go to our own
funeral. Then we come back singing: 'I am crucified with
Christ: nevertheless I live; yet not I, but Christ lives in
me.' Crucifixion with Christ is resurrection in yourself.
So don't see this challenge of Jesus as depressing or
imprisoning. It might appear like that at first, but the
rewards and benefits of denying self, and taking up the
cross, are much greater than the cost.

O Father, I see that when I am surrendered to You I don't
have to keep up appearances to prove anything. I simply
have to be my true self – in You. Amen.

Targeting the right people

FOR READING AND MEDITATION
MATTHEW 13:31–43

'I will open my mouth in parables, I will utter things hidden since the creation of the world.' (v.35)

I n college I was taught that there are five ways to teach. By cliché, by slogan, by proverb, by parable, by riddle. Clichés and slogans don't require much from listeners, but a proverb, a parable or a riddle, do. The art of teaching was to avoid clichés and slogans and put some responsibility upon listeners through the occasional use of proverbs, parables and riddles. Note that our Lord, particularly when speaking on the theme of discipleship, used a proverb, a parable or a riddle. These forms of teaching put pressure on listeners to think, ponder and reflect. This is because when it comes to understanding the things of God, it is not just a matter of IQ, but of faith, character and determination.

Beautiful, strong Son of God, I increasingly see that You are ultimate truth, ultimate reality and ultimate love. Where my treasure is, there my heart is also. I am at rest – in You. Amen.

The rate for the job

FOR READING AND MEDITATION
MATTHEW 20:1–16

'So the last will be first, and the first will be last.' (v.16)

This strange parable of Jesus constitutes another of His hard sayings, and one which offends many people, even today. A British trade union leader, when asked to read this passage in church, refused to do so because it appeared to defend the unacceptable principle of equal pay for unequal work. The main point of this parable is to stress the fact that God owes no one anything, and every benefit and reward He gives is essentially an act of grace. The arrangement did not seem fair to those who spent all day working in the vineyard, but only because they expected more even though they received what was agreed. We may not like it but the truth is this – those taken on at the last hour are going to be paid in full.

Father, is this really fair? My natural mind says 'no', but yet I know You can never be in the wrong. Teach me what You are saying to me through these words. Amen.

Significant boundaries

FOR READING AND MEDITATION
MATTHEW 19:16–30

'When the young man heard this, he went away sad, because he had great wealth.' (v.22)

This parable came about because of our Lord's conversation with the rich young man. Jesus said: 'Go, sell your possessions and give to the poor.' But the young man turned away. The thrust of Peter's question was this: 'We have left all to follow You; what then shall we have?' It was as if he had said, 'Lord, You called this man to a great renunciation and he failed. But *we* have left all to follow You. What shall we gain?' Jesus turned Peter's eyes to the future, and the rewards for His followers. The subject Jesus was illustrating, then, was service and its reward. The parable is not about salvation, but about rewards for those who are already saved. Miss this and the parable will remain a mystery.

Father, thank You for the way You stretch my mind in the interests of truth. But grant me continually the illuminating presence of Your Spirit. In Jesus' name. Amen.

God's generosity

FOR READING AND MEDITATION
DEUTERONOMY 15:1–18

*'Give generously to him and do so without a grudging
heart …' (v.10)*

Justice had been done for the labourers in the vineyard
because the original workers received what they were
promised – one denarius. Fairness is not the same as
justice. Many things God does appear unfair, but when we
look at those same issues from the angle of justice, then
the whole matter takes on a different perspective. The
point the owner of the vineyard makes to the labourers
who worked all day is this: 'If justice is done, have you
any right to object to my generosity?' That is the only
question that arises in connection with whether or not
the owner had a right to do what he liked with his own
money. The implication of the question in Jesus' parable
was that he had such a right. And so does God.

*Father, help me, when something happens to make me think
You are unfair, to set that against the bigger perspective
of Your unfailing justice so I see things from Your point of
view. Amen.*

Fidelity to opportunity

FOR READING AND MEDITATION
I CORINTHIANS 4:1–21

'Now it is required that those who have been given a trust must prove faithful.' (v.2)

What is Jesus really teaching in the parable of the labourers in the vineyard? The worker who was called in at the last hour never had a chance before. He had not been called, but when invited went in and was paid on the basis of the fact that for one hour he was faithful. The workman who went in at the beginning, and served through all the heat and burden of the day, was faithful to his work, and was paid accordingly. The parable, therefore, illustrates reward according to fidelity to opportunity. The Lord has called you and me into His vineyard. Only one thing ought to occupy us – that we do the job He gives us. When we do, then according to our fidelity will be our reward.

O Father, thank You for calling me to work in Your vineyard. I may have come in late but I know, provided I am faithful, I shall be paid in full. All honour and glory be to Your name. Amen.

Staying the course

FOR READING AND MEDITATION
2 TIMOTHY 4:1–8

'I have finished the race ... Now there is in store for me the crown of righteousness ...' (vv.7–8)

What opportunities has God given you? Are you closing in with them? Are you embracing them? He gave Billy Graham the opportunity of a worldwide ministry and, when his day's work is done, he will have his reward based on his fidelity to opportunity. There is a woman somewhere reading these lines who is trying to bring up her children single-handedly but she is doing everything she can to train them for God. Her name will never appear in the Christian magazines, but one day she, too, will get her reward. And when she does, she will be as full of joy as Billy Graham, for she will be paid on the same basis as he will be paid – faithfulness to opportunity. Mercifully, we receive God's love in *full*.

Father, thank You for this truth. Your love cannot be divided into parts, and thus Your payments are always in full. Amen.

One-legged law

FOR READING AND MEDITATION
MATTHEW 5:31–48

'Love your enemies and pray for those who persecute you ...' (v.44)

Jesus offended many by saying: 'Love your enemies.' The word used for love here is the strong Greek word *agape*. It means love that is unconditional, wholly unselfish, compassionate, generous, patient and forgiving. You can imagine how these words must have sounded to those who had been brought up on the law: 'An eye for an eye and a tooth for a tooth.' A sceptical Gentile once told a rabbi he would accept the Jewish faith if the rabbi could summarise the Jewish law while the Gentile stood on one leg. The rabbi replied: 'Do not do to another what would be hurtful to you.' Jesus, however, turned this on its head when He said: 'Do to others as you would have them do to you' (Luke 6:31).

Father, thank You for sending Your Son to show us the way of agape. For this is love that gives its all and then finds it all. May I receive and share that self-same agape love with others. Amen.

Get off your donkey

FOR READING AND MEDITATION
LUKE 10:25–37

'But he wanted to justify himself, so he asked Jesus, "And who is my neighbour?"' (v.29)

To the Jewish mind the Samaritans were worse than pagans. In turning a despised Samaritan into a hero, Jesus once again flipped the world of the Jews upside down. Jewish leaders acting without compassion, a vile Samaritan acting like a loving neighbour? What is Jesus trying to say here? He is pointing out the difference between law and *agape* love. *Agape* love is indiscriminate. It doesn't draw lines of responsibility and exclusion. *Agape* love is determined and bold; it doesn't allow religious custom to deter it. *Agape* love is expensive; it lends without thought of return. *Agape* love is the sign of the new kingdom, and our expression of it the sign that we are its subjects.

Jesus, thank You for Your agape. It is a love that never wears thin. I grow in the wonder of it, glory in the beauty of it, and surrender to the call of it. Now make me a channel of it. Amen.

The rule of reciprocity

FOR READING AND MEDITATION
MATTHEW 5:46–48

'If you love those who love you, what reward will you get?' (v.46)

The general view of love is that of reciprocity. The rule is this – we should appreciate things done for us and return people's favours. In the passage before us today Jesus cuts through this social norm and shows that *agape* love stretches far beyond the rule of reciprocity. *Agape* love is not returning smile for smile, or favour for favour – even sinners can live by that rule. Pharisees and tax collectors would smile at those who smiled at them. The Samaritan didn't play by the rule of reciprocity when he got off his donkey to help the injured traveller. He went beyond it to excess. The old law of 'tit for tat' is out; the new law of excess is in. It has been overtaken – by *agape*.

Father, I want to give as You give – with no strings attached, but giving with the excess of agape. *I have Your* agape, *now let others have it – through me. In Jesus' name. Amen.*

Equal doses

FOR READING AND MEDITATION
MATTHEW 22:34–46

'Love your neighbour as yourself.' (v.39)

The phrase 'love your neighbour as yourself' implies that it is appropriate and permissible to love oneself. There is a place for personal respect and dignity as long as we care for our neighbour to the same degree that we care for ourselves. As one writer puts it: 'Equal doses of self-love and neighbour-love flow from our ultimate love – devotion to God.' We are to love others as Jesus loved us (John 13:34–35). When we draw from God *agape* love then pride is immediately dislodged from within us and we care for our neighbour's welfare with the same intensity and passion that we care for our own. I find this terribly challenging but nevertheless I want it. Don't you?

Father, I am made for agape, and without it I function at less than my best. Show me even more clearly how to love You, love myself and love others. In Jesus' name I ask it. Amen.

Tough words!

FOR READING AND MEDITATION
LUKE 6:27–36

'Be merciful, just as your Father is merciful.' (v.36)

Jesus cut right across the idea of retaliation, and decreed that in the new kingdom enemies should be treated as friends. This kind of loving is bound to antagonise people, especially those who do not wish to make themselves vulnerable. But clearly, from Jesus' teaching, when we play by the old rules of retaliation then there is no Christian witness, no redemption. The willingness to suffer in the midst of injustice is something that very few can do without the aid of *agape* love. The message of Jesus, then, is blunt, clear and unequivocal – we love our enemies. Many Christians baulk at it, and some even reject it. His true disciples, however, believe it and by His strength demonstrate it wherever they go.

Father, give me Your strength, for there is no way I can demonstrate this kind of love on my own. You set the standard high, but then You lift me up to it. Amen.

Almost a lynching

FOR READING AND MEDITATION
LUKE 4:14–30

'I tell you the truth ... no prophet is accepted in his home town.' (v.24)

We look now at a saying of Jesus that almost got Him killed. Why did they try to throw Him off a hill? There were many widows in Israel in the time of Elijah, said Jesus, but Elijah was not helped in the years of famine by a Jewish widow, but by a Gentile one. Also, there were many lepers in Israel at the time of Elisha but it was Naaman, a Gentile, who was cleansed. These two stories sliced right through the people's Jewishness, their ethnicity, and showed them that belonging to the nation of Israel gave them no special rights to be helped by God or even healed by Him. In two simple stories Jesus said: 'The Gentiles are also loved by God.' His hearers' tribal pride was shattered – and they didn't like it.

O God, I am so thankful that Your love leaps over all geographical boundaries, and that there are no small or great in Your sight. You love each one of us as if there were only one to love. Amen.

God of outsiders

FOR READING AND MEDITATION
ISAIAH 61:1–11

'... to proclaim the year of the LORD's favour and the day
of vengeance of our God ...' (v.2)

In the eyes of the Jews, Gentiles were unclean; they
were pagans who contaminated the purity of the
Hebrew ceremonies. Jews went out of their way to avoid
Gentiles, whom they described as 'wild dogs'. It must
be noted that Jesus omitted a phrase at the end of the
Isaiah passage relating to the day of vengeance when
God would punish the wicked. The stories our Lord told
concerning Elijah and Elisha seemed to make the point
that in the new kingdom just about to be ushered in,
God would extend mercy and liberation even to the
'wicked' Gentiles. This was an offensive and scandalous
idea – something, as we have seen, our Lord was adept
at giving.

*Father, I rejoice that You are the God of the outsiders. I was,
as Scripture says, 'excluded from citizenship in Israel and
a foreigner to the covenant of promise', but You brought
me in. Amen.*

A Gentile's recognition

FOR READING AND MEDITATION
MARK 7:24–30

'Yes, Lord … but even the dogs under the table eat the children's crumbs.' (v.28)

In Mark's Gospel there are several symbolic signs of Gentiles being included in Christ's kingdom. Take just one – the Syro-Phoenician woman. Jesus uses a Jewish proverb: 'It is not right to take the children's bread and toss it to their dogs.' It is quite clear what He means when He uses the word 'dogs': He is referring to the Gentiles. She courageously turns His proverb back on Him and says: 'Yes, Lord, but even the dogs under the table eat the children's crumbs.' A Gentile, of all people, was calling Him 'Lord'. Astonished that she recognises His Lordship, He casts the demon out of her child. The demarcation lines between Jew and Gentile are being smudged by their being included together in the kingdom of God.

Lord Jesus, I see that those who are willing to be broken by You are those who are made whole by You. Thank You, my Saviour. Amen.

'Whoever will may come'

FOR READING AND MEDITATION
MATTHEW 8:1–13

'I tell you the truth, I have not found anyone in Israel with such great faith.' (v.10)

The Gentile army officer demonstrated greater faith than the religious leaders of Israel. We read Jesus said: 'Go home to your family and tell them how much the Lord has done for you, and how he has had mercy on you' (Mark 5:19). When Jesus healed Jews He usually told them not to tell anyone; when He healed a Gentile He bid him make the news known. Why? It can only be because He wanted the news spread among the Gentiles that the Jewish Messiah was here to minister to them also. The kingdom of God is multi-ethnic and crosses over all lines of demarcation. The social barricades that history had built between Jew and Gentile crumbled in the presence of Jesus of Nazareth. His message is: 'Whoever will may come.'

Father, what a gospel! May I spread the message in every way I can and wherever I go. Help me be alert, for today I might meet someone who is just waiting to be called by You. Amen.

One body!

FOR READING AND MEDITATION
I CORINTHIANS 12:12–27

'The body is a unit ... and though all its parts are many, they form one body.' (v.12)

We must relate to one another on the basis that every person who belongs to Christ also belongs to everyone else who belongs to Christ. We must work to demolish as many of the differences that exist among us as possible. Many of the labels we acquire outside of the Church follow us inside. This cannot be eliminated altogether, but we must be alert to the problems it presents. People may be doctors, nurses, secretaries, professors, students, businessmen or theologians, but these external labels must not be allowed to shape our relationships or interactions within the Church. A gospel that draws only people who are similar blurs the good news that bonds Jew and Gentile, male and female, black and white.

Father, drive this truth deeply into my spirit and into every one of the members of Your Church worldwide. Let there be no blurring of the good news in the Church of this century. Amen.

You can't get away

FOR READING AND MEDITATION
MATTHEW 6:1–18

'Be careful not to do your "acts of righteousness" before men, to be seen by them.' (v.1)

Another of the hard sayings of Jesus concerns religious practices. What really mattered to the religious leaders was how they appeared to others. When they prayed, they considered how their prayers would sound; when they gave, they made sure their giving was seen by others. Some sewed long fringes on their prayer shawls, symbolising the commandments, and sought the best seats on social occasions (Matt. 23:5–7; Luke 11:43; 20:46). Scribes said long prayers for the sake of social display (Mark 12:40; Luke 20:47). John even records the fact that some of the authorities who believed in Jesus were afraid to admit it because they loved the praise of men more than the praise of God (John 12:42–43).

Lord Jesus, grant that my passion for truth might come closer to Yours. Help me to confront issues with Your determination and love. Amen.

Compassion vs custom

FOR READING AND MEDITATION
MARK 2:18–28

'So the Son of Man is Lord even of the Sabbath.' (v.28)

Jesus respected the Sabbath, but He did not worship it; He worshipped God. The Sabbath was designed by God to serve people – to refresh them after six days of toil. It was never intended to be a master, but a servant. At other times He healed on the Sabbath day, showing that we must not put custom ahead of people's physical needs. Answering His critics on one such occasion, He noted that the Pharisees took better care of their animals than people (Matt. 12:9–13). They would pull a sheep out of a pit on the Sabbath, but not allow a doctor to minister to the sick. When religion became a ritual Jesus was against it. For Him compassion, not custom, was the rule.

Father, deliver me from the piety that would turn religion into a ritual. Help me understand that compassion must overrule custom, and that love must interpret law. In Jesus' name. Amen.

The heart of the matter

FOR READING AND MEDITATION
LUKE 11:37–54

'... the Pharisee, noticing that Jesus did not first wash before the meal, was surprised.' (v.38)

If Jesus came not to destroy the law but to fulfil it why did He ignore it? The answer lies in the difference between the written law and the oral law. Jesus endorsed the written law, but He scoffed at some aspects of the oral law – the rules that people had added to the written law over the centuries. The washing of hands before a meal was not done in order to wash away germs but to sanitise any religious 'dirt' that might have gathered during the day. In other words, it was a ritual. Jesus refrains from washing not because He is against the washing of hands before a meal, but to make the point that perfect cleansing does not occur in a ritual but in acts of love flowing out of the heart.

Father, I see that in Your eyes the heart of the matter is always the matter of the heart. Save me from falling into the trap that the Pharisees fell into of outer cleanliness but inner dirt. Amen.

Friend of sinners

FOR READING AND MEDITATION
MARK 2:13–17

'I have not come to call the righteous, but sinners.' (v.17)

The Pharisees were offended by the way Jesus related to 'sinners'. To invite someone to a meal was to honour him. It was a sign of trust, intimacy and forgiveness. To share one's table meant to share one's life. They said: 'This man welcomes sinners and eats with them' (Luke 15:2). By eating with those whom religion rejected, Jesus showed His compassion for all types of humanity. Jesus made the point that in His kingdom all are invited, regardless of their condition or even the depth of their sin. He showed that people are more important than pious religious rules. It is a sign of their acceptance at the heavenly banquet table, provided of course they turn from their sin and receive Him as their Saviour.

Jesus, how can I ever thank You sufficiently for the love that embraces all? Were it not that kind of love then I would not be in Your kingdom today. You are such a loving Friend to me. Amen.

'A den of robbers'

FOR READING AND MEDITATION
MARK 11:1–19

'My house will be called a house of prayer for all nations.'
(v.17)

Keep in mind that the Temple was the hub of Jewish worship. It was one thing to berate the Pharisees for their oral traditions; it was quite another to enter the Temple and boldly challenge the authority of the priestly families who allowed these things to go on for their personal gain. Mark, in his Gospel, shows how the plot to kill Jesus gathered momentum as a result of this incident. Note, however, that what Jesus is against here is not Jewish religion but human religion, or rather human activity abusing true faith. He cleansed the Temple not because it was Jewish, but corrupt. What would He do if He stood in some of today's churches where prayer and spirituality are low priorities? I wonder!

Lord Jesus, help me understand that you were not against piety as such, but impious piety. Teach me ever to discern the difference between the two. Amen.

The money test

FOR READING AND MEDITATION
LUKE 16:1–15

'The Pharisees, who loved money, heard all this and were sneering at Jesus.' (v.14)

We turn now to the last of our Lord's hard sayings concerning the subject He talked about most – money. Jesus made the issue of money basic to His kingdom. He expects every one of His disciples to have the right attitude to money. Our Lord is not against us owning things; what He is against is when we allow them to own us. He didn't say material things are inherently evil, but He did warn of their danger. Money, possessions and material things can quickly become demons that unseat the rule of God. This is why those who wish to be Christ's disciples must have a clear focus on this subject. We cannot serve God and mammon, but we can serve God with mammon.

Father, a real battle goes on in some hearts when the issue of money is mentioned. Perhaps even in mine. We are victims of false values, false goals, false ideas. Help us come to sanity. Amen.

Who is master?

FOR READING AND MEDITATION
JAMES 4:1–17

'Now listen, you who say, "Today or tomorrow we will ... carry on business and make money."' (v.13)

The values of Christ's kingdom clash with the economic values of almost every age – ours included. Jesus never cut more deeply into the hearts of His listeners than when He challenged them about their possessions. His call for a sense of stewardship and generosity in material things shook the economic structures that encouraged huge disparities between the rich and the poor. He made it clear that working hard for money did not justify someone spending it lavishly and selfishly. He warned that the acquisitive streak in human nature could turn into a powerful god, capturing the imagination, demanding total allegiance. People could finish by bending their knees not to God, but to gold.

O Father, I see that although money and possessions can be good servants, they can also be terrible masters. Grant that I might be mastered only by You. Amen.

Be warned!

FOR READING AND MEDITATION
LUKE 12:13–34

'This is how it will be with anyone who stores up things for himself but is not rich towards God.' (v.21)

Jesus taught that there are six dangers to consider in relation to this matter of material possessions. First, possessions, if we let them, can strangle our spiritual lives (Luke 8:14). Second, they can be a cause for constant worry (Luke 12:22–24). Third, they can blind (Luke 16:19–23). Fourth, they can become our boss (Luke 16:1–9). Fifth, they can damn (Luke 12:13–21). Sixth, they can curse (Luke 6:20, 24). These six things can undercut our allegiance to God's kingdom, and so we must be careful that we do not allow ourselves to be tied too closely to our possessions. Preoccupation with material things can choke and stifle our spiritual lives and open us to anxiety. Be warned.

O God, I hear Your warnings and pray now that You will help me get this matter of material values straightened out in my mind. In Jesus' name. Amen.

The Gift of gifts!

FOR READING AND MEDITATION
2 CORINTHIANS 9:1–15

'Thanks be to God for his indescribable gift!' (v.15)

Five important issues flow from our Lord's teaching on money. First, He directs us again and again to give to the poor. Second, our generosity must overflow to other Christians who are in need. Third, we must not exploit people and take from them more than we ought. Fourth, giving money to the needy does not release us from the responsibility of giving time in prayer, advice, education, and so on. Money sometimes isn't enough. Fifth, giving to others ought to bring spiritual as well as material liberation. Without this biblical perspective, financial aid to people simply affects them materially. Our giving ought to draw attention to Jesus, God's greatest gift.

Father, I am coming under the sway of Your creative Spirit. You are sensitising my inmost being to Yours. May I, like You, be a generous giver. Amen.

Give! Give! Give!

FOR READING AND MEDITATION
MATTHEW 10:1–16

'Freely you have received, freely give.' (v.8)

It is so easy to be brainwashed by the world's systems and values that we miss the way of the Master in relation to this matter of money. For example, is it morally right to pay only a minimum wage even when it is legal? Is charging the highest price the market can stand the right way to go about business? What we must not do as Christians is to assume that the way things are is the right way. Disciples are radical. And if ever we needed Radicalism it is now. We need to find creative ways to use our resources on behalf of the poor, give beyond people's expectations, give more than a tithe, surprise people by our generosity. It all sounds upside down doesn't it? But then, this is an upside-down kingdom.

Father, You have Your finger on the nerve centre of my life. Help me face these challenges for I see that they are weighty and important issues. I want to be a faithful steward and disciple. Amen.

All the way

FOR READING AND MEDITATION
LUKE 5:1–11

'So they pulled their boats up on shore, left everything and followed him.' (v.11)

Our Lord is looking not for adherents to His cause, or 'hangers-on', but out-and-out disciples. To be made whole and wholly follow Him means that we must first be broken on Him; He is, after all, 'the stone that causes men to stumble'. Mark Twain spoke for many when he said that the things in the Bible that bothered him were not those he did not understand, but those he did understand. This is particularly true concerning the hard sayings of Jesus. The better we understand them, the harder they are to take. F.F. Bruce says that this may be one of the reasons why people resist modern translations of the Bible, as the clearer things are, the more challenging they become.

Father, I want to go all the way with You no matter what the cost. Make me one of Your true disciples. In Jesus' name I pray. Amen.

New wineskins

FOR READING AND MEDITATION
MATTHEW 9:9–17

'… men … pour new wine into new wineskins …' (v.17)

Our next theme comes from the apostle Paul's triumphant phrase found in the eighth chapter of Romans: 'We are more than conquerors through him who loved us' (8:37). Paul did not say: 'We are conquerors through him who loved us', but he put in the added emphasis: 'more than conquerors'. The early Christians had to lay hold on one superlative after another in order to convey the wondrous truths originating from our Lord's coming into the world. The new wine had not only to be put into the new wineskins of organisation and ministry, but also into the new wineskins of a new vocabulary. Here was a fresh, new set of facts. To be a conqueror is one thing, to be *more* than a conqueror is another.

Father, I see that this is one 'more' that really counts. May I learn how to avail myself of all the resources available to me in Christ. Amen.

Old word – new content

FOR READING AND MEDITATION
JOHN 15:9–25

'Love each other as I have loved you.' (v.12)

The early Christians had to adapt old words to express their faith. Anders Nygren, an authority on the use of Greek words, says: 'In ancient times two men commented about God: Plato – "God is *eros*"; John – "God is Agape". Just the difference of two words but behind them the difference of two worlds.' Over the centuries *eros* has come to be associated with sexual love, and *agape* with the love of the Deity. This is because a Christian content has been put into *agape;* a word that in its original usage was distinctly human has become one of the best vehicles for expressing the love that flows down to us from heaven. When we think of *eros* we think of Plato; when we think of *agape* we think of Jesus.

Father, I see that eros *has a place, but there is more to love than* eros. *There is* agape. *May Your* agape *create* agape *in me. Amen.*

'Disorganised grammar'

FOR READING AND MEDITATION
EPHESIANS 3:1–21

'Now to him who is able to do immeasurably more than all we ask or imagine …' (v.20)

Look how the New King James Version puts our text for today: 'Now to Him who is able to do exceedingly abundantly above all we ask or think …' 'Exceedingly abundantly' – this phrase comes much closer to the thought in the original Greek. You get the feeling that Paul, as he writes, is leaping over all boundaries, widening all horizons, blowing away all restrictions, in an effort to enable us to see how good and great God is. One theologian who made a study of the language of the early disciples says that there are times when their passion resulted in the disorganisation of their grammar. Sometimes grammatical rules can't bear the pressure of this new, glorious, effervescent life.

O Father, sometimes the reality of what You have done for me in Jesus becomes so overwhelming that words become inadequate. This new wine needs new wineskins! Amen.

Moral winners

FOR READING AND MEDITATION
PHILIPPIANS 4:10–23

'I can do everything through him who gives me strength.'
(v.13)

I tried by sheer willpower to break the bad habits in my life, but they beat me every time. Since I gave my life to Jesus Christ I have been conscious of a new-found power at work within me that carries me past the temptations that I once fell prey to. What does it mean to be *more* than a conqueror? I love the explanation of the little boy in Sunday school who, when asked that question, replied: 'To be a conqueror means to win by fighting; to be more than a conqueror means to win without fighting.' Well, it is not a perfect explanation – the Christian life is not passivity – but it is a good enough starting point. We are moral winners because we have the Moral Winner – within.

Father, the extra resources I have in You provide me with the possibility of being a moral winner. In You I can do more than I did before because I have more than I had before. Amen.

Non-expectancy

FOR READING AND MEDITATION
REVELATION 1:1–8

'… to him be glory and power for ever and ever!' (v.6)

During a conference at which I spoke, one speaker said: 'The chief characteristic of modern-day Christianity is non-expectancy.' I remember thinking: I hope what he says is not true because if it is then the situation is deadly serious. When we expect nothing to happen, nothing will. Those of us who live in the West have watched what the awful power of fatalism can do to some other areas of the world when talented and capable people turn over their hands in helpless resignation. But what is worse is to see Christians settle down in a spirit of non-expectancy and live out their lives in spiritual and moral defeat. Many Christians do not even see themselves as conquerors, let alone more than conquerors.

O God, forgive me if the vivacity, the sparkle, and the joy that should characterise a Christian, are not to be found in my heart. Help me to live abundantly. In Jesus' name. Amen.

Naturalised in defeat

FOR READING AND MEDITATION
ROMANS 15:1–13

'… that you may overflow with hope by the power of the Holy Spirit.' (v.13)

C an it be that we have people in today's Church who think that being spiritually strong is something strange and unnatural? One doctor said: 'When I tell them [Christians] that this condition of moral and spiritual defeat need not last, that they can find victory and adequacy and buoyancy in living, they look at me as one who announces a strange doctrine. They have become naturalised in defeat.' Many Christians do not expect anything beyond repeated forgiveness for constantly repeated sins. They certainly do not expect victory over them. This attitude of non-expectancy is something that must be confronted. Christians must never allow themselves to become naturalised in defeat.

My Father and my God, You are putting Your finger on our need. Help us to press against the gates of abundant living and enter into Your victory. Save us from becoming naturalised in defeat. Amen.

Pardon and power

FOR READING AND MEDITATION
ROMANS 8:1–8

'... the law of the Spirit of life set me free from the law of sin and death.' (v.2)

Is constant forgiveness for constantly repeated sin the best we can expect? If so, then Christianity offers pardon, but with no power. We need both if we are to represent the gospel of our Lord Jesus Christ. The gospel does offer forgiveness for sin, but along with it, and as a part of it, it also offers the power to overcome sin. Forgiveness and power are the indissoluble parts of the grace of God. We cannot take one without the other. If we tried to take the forgiveness without the power then we would be faced with moral weakness. If we tried to take the power without the forgiveness then we would be faced with moral guilt. God does not give one without the other. We must take both, or neither.

Father, what a joy it is to know that in You I find not only forgiveness for all the sins of the past, but power to overcome sin in the future. Amen.

No immunity!

FOR READING AND MEDITATION
JAMES 1:1–18

'... *God cannot be tempted by evil, nor does he tempt anyone ...*' (v.13)

B efore we go on to look at what it means in practical terms to be 'more than a conqueror', we must look at what it does not mean. First, *it does not mean that we will be immune to temptation*. It is not the temptation that produces sin, but the desires within us that go unchecked and uncontrolled. Temptation, therefore, is not sin; only when we yield to it does it become sin. No one can stop the suggestion of evil entering the mind, but we can stop harbouring it and brooding over it. Jesus went into the wilderness to be tempted of the devil but came through the experience 'without sin'. Being 'more than a conqueror', then, does not mean being immune to temptation, but being a victor over it.

Lord Jesus, You came through the wilderness of temptation stronger than when You went in. Walk with me into my struggles and cause me to do the same. Amen.

'Purity is not maturity'

FOR READING AND MEDITATION
I SAMUEL 16:1–13

'Man looks at the outward appearance, but the LORD looks at the heart.' (v.7)

Being 'more than a conqueror' *does not imply freedom from mistakes.* We must never forget that we are personalities in the making. This does not mean we must lower the standards, but it does mean that sometimes we will make mistakes. Our intentions may be very good, but because our intelligence is limited, the action may result in a mistake – a mistake but not necessarily a sin. One theologian says: 'Purity is not maturity.' When my children were very young one of them wrote me a letter. It was covered with ink blots, and contained a number of mistakes. Was it mature? No. Was it pure? Yes. I saw through the immaturity to the intention and that made all the difference. It is the same with God.

Father, this gospel of Yours is called the Way. Our feet are on the Way, but only on the way – we have not arrived at our goal. Help me to walk on that way always. Amen.

Crying for the Shepherd

FOR READING AND MEDITATION
ISAIAH 55:1–13

'… turn to the LORD, and he will have mercy … and to
our God, for he will freely pardon.' (v.7)

B eing 'more than a conqueror' does not mean freedom
from mistakes; *it does not mean, either, that we never
again commit a wrong act or sin.* We must not forget
that there is provision for us when we sin. We are not
to concentrate on that provision, but we are to partake
of it whenever necessary. One of the differences between
a sheep and a pig is that when a sheep falls into a mud
hole it bleats until it gets out. When a pig falls into a
mud hole it loves it, delights in it and would wallow
in it forever. True and growing Christians are those who
go out into the day availing themselves of the power to
overcome sin. And if they sin they do not sink deeper
into the mud but cry out for the Shepherd.

*Father, help me to get my perspective right – the victory
available and the provision for sin. Help me to think not
so much that it is possible to sin, but that it is possible not
to sin. Amen.*

A spiritual dyarchy

FOR READING AND MEDITATION
I JOHN 5:1–5

'… everyone born of God overcomes the world.' (v.4)

B eing 'more than a conqueror' means, quite simply, that we allow Christ to reign in every portion of our being and in all our relationships. Many Christians allow Christ to function in certain areas of their lives while other areas are withheld. Over these special or reserved areas we rule, we make the decisions. This, of course, introduces the principle of duality into life – something that works to produce inner division. In India, many years ago, the British arranged to have certain 'reserved subjects' while turning the others over to the Indians. That kind of government was called a 'dyarchy'. Inevitably, the system failed, just as the attempt to have a spiritual dyarchy within the soul will fail.

Lord Jesus Christ, forgive us that we have thought to make You a half-king, leaving other half-gods in our hearts. We cannot bow at a double shrine. Forgive us and help us. Amen.

Duality brings disaster

FOR READING AND MEDITATION
REVELATION 3:14–22

'… you are neither cold nor hot. I wish you were either one or the other!' (v.15)

Some people have only enough of the love of Christ in their hearts to make them miserable. They do not enjoy a spiritual life or an unspiritual life. If we do not allow Christ to enter into the very core of our beings and take over the control room of our lives, then His presence in some parts of our lives, and not in others, creates a war between the opposing ideas of life and we live in a state of internal war. This tension does not always become apparent to the conscious mind, but it is certainly apparent to the unconscious mind. The point is there can be no real happiness in the heart of someone who has reserved areas into which Christ is not invited. Duality cannot exist in the soul without disaster.

Father, I am thankful that You claim the whole of my heart and not just a part. I surrender all to You so You may be Lord of all. Amen.

Why do we struggle?

FOR READING AND MEDITATION
ROMANS 7:7–25

'What a wretched man I am! Who will rescue me from this body of death?' (v.24)

Why is it that we resist surrendering every area of our lives to Jesus Christ? Largely, it is because we like things to be under our control. The sin Adam and Eve committed in the Garden of Eden was a declaration of independence. We like to be in control of the way our lives work. Becoming a victorious Christian involves a complete and total surrender of the ego to Jesus, and the willingness not to continue living as an ego-centred person but a Christ-centred one. Who doesn't prefer to hold on to the visible securities of life even when they are in shreds? We fear that in having Him we might have naught beside. What fools we are not to believe He is enough.

O God, will I ever be free of the insanity that puts visible security before the Invisible? May I come to trust You more than I trust the things I can touch and see. In Jesus' name. Amen.

'In all things'

FOR READING AND MEDITATION
ISAIAH 41:1–16

'… do not fear, for I am with you; do not be dismayed,
for I am your God.' (v.10)

Scripture says: '… in all these things we are more
than conquerors …'(Rom. 8:37). The words 'in all
these things' bring an intense realism to what otherwise
might be seen as mere optimism. I say 'realism' for in
the Christian faith there is no evasion of the difficulties
that confront victorious living. Those Christians who
handle life by pretending there are no problems are
simply building their houses on sand. Any attempt to
establish life on the sands of denial rather than on the
rock of reality is doomed to failure. Denial is an attempt
to dethrone God. It assumes that God is not quite big
enough to handle whatever we are called upon to face,
so we distort reality to accommodate our unbelief.

*O God, forgive me if denial is one of the techniques I use
to survive. Give me such a vision of Yourself that I will be
able to face anything that comes. Amen.*

The way of realism

FOR READING AND MEDITATION
JOHN 17:1–19

'My prayer is not that you take them out of the world but that you protect them from the evil one.' (v.15)

The things Paul mentions in Romans 8:35–39 are not pleasant or agreeable, but deeply upsetting: 'trouble, hardship, persecution, famine, nakedness, danger, or sword'. True spirituality must include the world of the physical and material. That is the test. The Buddhists say we must be *indifferent* to all things. The Muslim term is *beyond* all things. The Hindu term is *apart* from all things. The Communist attitude was *through* all things. The word used in some modern cults is *deny* all things. Hedonists say *by* all things. Every one of these formulae wants victory apart from these things. Christians want victory in all these things. This makes the Christian way the way of realism, not idealism.

Thank You my Father that You put the Christian victory where it is reachable and attainable – right in the midst of things. In You I can conquer in everything. Amen.

'Ten horses of evil'

FOR READING AND MEDITATION
ROMANS 8:28—39

' … will be able to separate us from the love of God that is in Christ Jesus our Lord.' (v.39)

Paul identifies ten things that cannot separate us from the love of God. When he calls the role call of these ten things he is not intending to limit the Christian victory to just these possibilities. In reality, he is saying: 'Nothing can break you if you do not break with Him.' Someone has called these the 'ten horses of evil' that try to ride us down and trample us under their feet until we arrive in a place of doubt and despair. We must learn, however, that we need not let them ride us down. Instead, we should grasp their bridles, swing into their saddles and ride them to our own destination of greater faith. When we learn how to do that we are learning not just to live, but to live victoriously.

Father, thank You that nothing can separate me from Your love. Teach me to let difficulties draw me deeper into Your love and not ride away from You. Amen.

'Room to grow up in'

FOR READING AND MEDITATION
1 CORINTHIANS 15:12–28

'The last enemy to be destroyed is death.' (v.26)

We consider the first horse of evil – death. Some people refuse to discuss the subject of death because it produces feelings in them they would rather not confront. An old Christian lady used to say: 'I look forward to death and immortality for I want room to grow up in.' She lived in the deathless One and was therefore, in a sense, deathless. To be freed from the fear of death is freedom indeed, for it is one of the greatest personal fears. However, for many people ongoing life holds unnamed terrors. We need power not only to stand up to life, but to be more than a conqueror in it. Remember that life holds nothing that Christ has not conquered. If you are a Christian, you are possessed by unconquerable Life.

O God, I see that nothing need make me afraid. I am possessed by Life; what can life do to me? In You I am ready for anything. Amen.

Seeing good as evil

FOR READING AND MEDITATION
EPHESIANS 1:3–23

'… far above all rule and authority, power and dominion …' (v.21)

When Paul says that angels might separate us from the love of God I think he sees that angels represent the good things of life that come to us – love, joy, happiness, prosperity, friends, and so on. Some people I have met have been more afraid of good things than bad things. They were so filled with self-despising and self-hate that they could not conceive that they were worthy of receiving good things and using them victoriously. In some strange way they saw good things as evil. Paul also lists demons. No demon, however bold or strong, can separate a Christian from God's love. Every one of them is on a leash. And the leash is in the nail-scarred hands of the One who engineered their defeat at Calvary.

Father, help me lay everything at Your feet – the prosperity as well as the penury, the joy as well as the sorrow. In Jesus' name I pray. Amen.

How never to be old

FOR READING AND MEDITATION
ISAIAH 46:1–13

'Even to your old age and grey hairs … I … will sustain you.' (v.4)

The next item on Paul's list is: 'neither the present'. 'Things present' in your life may be difficult or monotonous but they do not have any terror, for you do not belong to them; you belong to Him. You receive the creative spirit of Christ, and you are able to make all things serve. After 'the present' Paul adds 'the future'. Millions are afraid of the future, particularly the idea of growing old. People should be taught how to grow old, just as we teach young people to grow up. The secret is never to retire from life, by continuing to be active and maybe taking up new interests. There is a stimulus in Christ that puts a sparkle into life and makes it creative amid the uncreative.

O God, I am thankful for the years that come and go and, above all, I am thankful for the possibility that they can grow more beautiful and blessed. Amen.

Trouble with authority?

FOR READING AND MEDITATION
MARK 12:1–17

'Give to Caesar what is Caesar's and to God what is God's.' (v.17)

Continuing our study of the things that might make us think they have the power to separate us from the love of God, we come to: 'nor any powers'. We do not know precisely what Paul was thinking about, but most probably he had in mind the powers that are over us in authority. A political power, for example, or even a dominant person. Then the next point: 'neither height'. We can never rise to a height where we can go beyond God's loving reach. The psalmist had the same thought in Psalm 139:7–8 when he said: 'Where can I go from your Spirit? Where can I flee from your presence? If I go up to the heavens, you are there …' God's love spans the whole of creation; there is nowhere where it is not.

Father, I see so clearly that 'the powers that be' lose their power over me when I am gripped and held by Your power. Amen.

'Nor anything else'

FOR READING AND MEDITATION
JUDE 3–25

'Keep yourselves in God's love …' (v.21)

'**N**or depth'. However far we descend into the depths, God's love has gone lower still. A submarine commander I met some years ago told me that he had found Christ at the bottom of the sea. 'I was lying in my bunk in a submarine on a three-day exercise at the bottom of the ocean,' he said. '… I lifted my heart upwards to God in a prayer of repentance and I was instantly saved.' Some commentators apply this thought of the 'depths' to the depths of depression. God's love reaches even there. Paul finally adds: 'nor anything else in all creation'. Nothing, absolutely nothing, can separate us from the love of God in Christ Jesus our Lord. Thus we can be more than conquerors.

My Father and my God, the scene is set for victory. Life holds nothing that Your love cannot conquer. I have taken hold of this truth; now let it take hold of me. Amen.

The basis of certainty

FOR READING AND MEDITATION
2 TIMOTHY 1:1–18

'God [has given us] a spirit of power, of love and of self-discipline.' (v.7)

Look how the Amplified Bible translates today's text: 'For God did not give us a spirit of timidity – of cowardice, of craven and clinging and fawning fear – but He has given us a spirit of power and of love and of calm and a well-balanced mind and discipline and self-control.' Here, then, is the basis of being 'more than a conqueror': the whole organism is strengthened. The will, the emotions and mind are renewed. There is power for the will, love for the emotions, and sound judgment for the mind. What more could one want in order to cope with life? When the will, emotions and mind are under the control of Christ, then all fear is banished. It is the answer of His Life to our inadequate life.

Father, I invite You to take possession of my will, my emotions and my mind. Take them all in Your hands and remake me in the image of Your Son. Amen.

Fear – the thing to fear

FOR READING AND MEDITATION
JEREMIAH 30:1–17

'So do not fear ... do not be dismayed ...' (v.10)

Some fears contribute to our efficiency and wellbeing. Fear, after all, is the best policeman on our traffic-infested roads. The fears I am concerned with here, however, are the fears that paralyse and incapacitate us. I can never forget a wildlife film I once saw that showed a small bird sitting on the branch of a tree being mesmerised by the eyes of a large cobra. It sat there crouched in fear before the cobra's overarching hood. Fear had paralysed it and made it an easy prey. No Christian need be paralysed by fear. Aware of it perhaps, even apprehensive, but never its prey. Whatever the fear, if it hinders a Christian's functioning, then it simply has to go.

God my Father, whatever fears may be at work from without or within me, give me the inner resources to be able to stand up to them – fearless and unafraid. In Jesus' name. Amen.

'The great destroyer'

FOR READING AND MEDITATION
MATTHEW 25:14–30

'So I was afraid and went out and hid your talent in the ground.' (v.25)

A story tells of a traveller who crossed a desert and met another traveller coming from the opposite direction who identified himself as *Cholera*. Cholera named the city that he had just left. The traveller said: 'How many died?' 'Eighty thousand,' Cholera replied, 'but I touched only twenty thousand.' 'And the rest?' 'Oh, they died from fear.' Today's passage informs us of a man whose efficiency and effectiveness were curbed because of fear. How many Christians, I wonder, will go out into the world today and fail to increase the spiritual investment that the Master, our Lord Jesus Christ, has deposited within them, due to some incapacitating fear? In Christ we must gain the victory over all such fear.

O Father, teach me how to take the first steps on this road to victory over fear. And teach me, also, to walk forever on it. Amen.

What compels us?

FOR READING AND MEDITATION
2 CORINTHIANS 5:11–21

'For Christ's love compels us, because we are convinced that one died for all …' (v.14)

It has to be said that many of us carry all kinds of repressed fears in our unconscious, but these fears seldom hinder us from functioning in life, except, perhaps, on rare occasions. What is to be done with these fears? If they do not have any disabling impact upon us – nothing. The fears that have to be looked at are those that lay a paralysing hand upon our activities and hinder effective personal functioning. When fear stops us being our best for God then that fear ought to be confronted and brought into His presence. As Christians we are to be compelled not by fear, but by love.

O God, I know I have no business being driven by fear when You are my Redeemer. Take from within me all basis of fear. I ask this in the victorious name of Jesus. Amen.

Expand yourself!

FOR READING AND MEDITATION
1 JOHN 4:7–21

'There is no fear in love. But perfect love drives out fear …' (v.18)

To be 'more than conquerors' we must know how to conquer every paralysing fear. But how? First, by admitting the things of which we are afraid. Denial does not work. Next, we must see that all fears are rooted in one thing – inner division. The inwardly united soul, that is, the person whose will, emotions and mind are held in the grip of Christ, knows no paralysing fear. Expand your personality through perfect love so that love empowers the will, drives the emotions and clears the mind. This expansion drives out all fear. The answer of the gospel is in line with its own nature – it is positive, affirmative, revolutionary and expansive.

Father, all I need give is myself to be free from paralysing fears. You have given Yourself unreservedly to me. Help me to give myself unreservedly to You. Amen.

Unafraid!

FOR READING AND MEDITATION
GENESIS 3:1–19

'I heard you in the garden, and I was afraid because I was naked; so I hid.' (v.10)

If all fears are rooted in one thing – inner division – it follows, then, that the remedy for fear lies in a unified self – a self made whole by Christ. Perfect love literally does cast out fear just as, vice versa, imperfect love literally admits fear into the heart. Before Adam sinned he was a whole person, enjoying the flow of God's eternal love. When, by wilful disobedience, he put up a barrier to that love, the first thing that swept into his heart was fear. But our love for Christ fuses the divisions of the soul into a burning unity. There is no room for inner fear, for there is no room for inner division. Our soul belongs to the One who is afraid of nothing – hence it is unafraid.

Lord Jesus Christ, You who conquered everything, conquer now my inner being. For when I am conquered by You then I can conquer anything. Amen.

'Listen to Him!'

FOR READING AND MEDITATION
MATTHEW 17:1–13

'Jesus … said, "Don't be afraid." When they looked up, they saw no-one except Jesus.' (vv.7–8)

There can be no conquest of fear unless there is an undivided and single loyalty to Christ. This is vividly brought home to us in the transfiguration scene. The Jewish heart of Peter was divided in its loyalty – wanting to keep Moses representing the law, Elijah representing the prophets, and Jesus representing the new revelation. But it is only Jesus Peter should listen to. When Jesus is not central then fear rises – inevitably. God's voice is speaking to us today as surely as it did on the transfiguration mount, and it is saying the same thing: 'This is my Son, whom I love … Listen to him.' Believe me, the fears will never depart until we do listen to Christ and make Him the Lord of our lives.

O God, You are speaking today in response to our inner divisions and confused loyalties. You are trying to show us that Jesus is the only One who can save us. We will listen to Him. Amen.

The greatest pain

FOR READING AND MEDITATION
ROMANS 8:9–17

'For you did not receive a spirit that makes you a slave again to fear …' (v.15)

A strong conviction of mine is that the greatest pain in the personality is the pain one experiences when one does not feel loved. And because this is the greatest pain, the greatest fear is the fear of being unloved. Now because of the final act of giving Himself for us on the cross, we know God loves us – loves us not because we are deserving and worthy, but because He can do nothing else but love. Nothing in us gave rise to it, and nothing in us can extinguish it. He loves, full stop. Many Christians have got hold of the truth of God's love, but it has not got hold of them. They understand it, but they have not learned to stand upon it. The power lies in getting it from our heads into our souls.

O Father, I see that one of the greatest pains the soul can feel – the pain of being unloved – need never be mine. Help me not just understand this, but stand on it. Amen.

Where love starts

FOR READING AND MEDITATION
ROMANS 5:1–11

'God demonstrates his own love for us in this: While we were still sinners, Christ died for us.' (v.8)

Faith is a by-product of love, a result of the invasion of divine love into our hearts. The moment I begin to love His love, that moment I begin to love with His love. I love God with the love of God. And I love others with the love of God. God has loved me into loving, and into loving with His love. Once we grasp the fact that He loves us regardless, then that love produces love in us in return. 'We love because he first loved us' (1 John 4:19). It is not our love for Him that drives away fear, but His love for us. That love awakens a love in us, and we begin to love in response, begin to love Him and love others. His love begets love in me. This is the heart of our faith.

O Divine Lover of my soul, I see that the love that rises in me is in direct proportion to the amount of love that I allow into me. Help me open my whole being to Your love. Amen.

One burning message

FOR READING AND MEDITATION
GALATIANS 2:11–21

'I have been crucified with Christ and I no longer live, but Christ lives in me.' (v.20)

It is not our love for Christ that rids us of fear and weakness, but His love for us. One message that burns within me constantly, and comes out in all my writings, is this: 'If you think your problem is that you do not love the Lord enough then think again, for you have got it the wrong way round. Your problem is you don't know how much the Lord loves you.' Love begins and continues in the Christian heart when we allow His love (*agape*) to strike ours and create the same degree of love (*agape*) in us. A downhearted missionary tells when she saw in a new way how much she was loved by God, immediately her attitude changed. Where there was revulsion for sinners now came a tender love and concern.

My Father and my God, I am grateful that I do not have to strive to love. I simply have to allow Love to love me into loving. Help me grasp this truth I pray. Amen.

An open heart

FOR READING AND MEDITATION
1 JOHN 3:1–20

'This is how we know what love is: Jesus Christ laid down his life for us.' (v.16)

You are not afraid of people you love; you are afraid of people you don't love. Commissioner Brengle said: 'I opened my heart to the love of God and He gave me such a blessing I never dreamed a man could have this side of heaven. Oh how I loved. In that hour I knew Jesus and I loved till it seemed my heart would break with love. I loved the sparrows. I loved the dogs. I loved the horses. I loved little urchins on the street. I loved the world.' Strengthened and empowered by such love there is no fear of anybody, anything, or any situation. The secret of Commissioner Brengle's passion is found in the words: 'I opened my heart to the love of God …' God's love cannot come in unless we let it in.

O Father, I realise I am not the spring of love, but its channel. Help me open myself more fully than ever to the great Niagara of Your love. Now and for ever. Amen.

The reason for living

FOR READING AND MEDITATION
REVELATION 1:1–20

'… To him who loves us and has freed us from our sins by his blood …' (v.5)

An old song says, 'Love is my reason for living'. Without love there is just no point to our existence, and certainly no power to overcome life's great fears. If we do not open our beings to the love of God so that He flows in to quicken us and inflame us with His passion, then we can never be unified personalities. Where there is no love our minds will lack a sound and unified judgment. We will fear intellectual inadequacy. If we do not love God supremely we become uncomfortable at the thought of Him. We do not love His will, and so we are apprehensive about what He might ask us to do. If there is no love for God there can be no real love for life, because life can only have meaning as He is in it.

Father, one thing is certain – fear and love cannot co-exist. I choose Your way, the way of love. Let Your love flow in until every fear flows out. Amen.

The core issue

FOR READING AND MEDITATION
JOHN 15:1–17

'If a man remains in me and I in him, he will bear much fruit ...' (v.5)

The crucial issue underlying the ability to be 'more than a conqueror' is for our lives to be organised around love. Matters such as faith, self-discipline, prayer, the regular reading of the Scriptures, play a part too, but the core issue is love. The more the love of God, as expressed in our Lord and Saviour Jesus Christ, permeates our personalities, the more our powers are heightened. The mind becomes keener and more creative, the emotions deeper and more sensitive, the will more active and decisive. The whole of life becomes outreaching. This is because love is creative, and when the love of God is the driving force of our personalities, the movement of our lives is also creative.

O God, how can I ever thank You sufficiently for the creative impact of Your love? Make me creative this day as I come in contact with dull, dead Godless life. Amen.

Love is creative

FOR READING AND MEDITATION
JOHN 7:25–39

'Whoever believes in me ... streams of living water will flow from within him.' (v.38)

Because divine love is creative then we ought to look for it to be at work in our lives and be ready to give expression to it. It's astonishing how we go through task after task in the same old way when, with a little thought and creativity, the most mundane tasks can be done in different and more inventive ways. The creativity I am talking about here is not innate creativity, for I recognise that some have more of this than others. However, when we are in contact with the world's most aggressive Lover, whose love spills over into creativity, then something of that ought to rub off on us – if we let it. People who are loved are people who love, and love is nothing if not creative.

Father, Your love has impacted my life in the most creative way. Now may Your love flowing through me impact others in the same creative way. Amen.

Conquered – to conquer

FOR READING AND MEDITATION
ACTS 20:13–38

'… we must help the weak, remembering the words … "It is more blessed to give than to receive."' (v.35)

Another way in which the conquering Christ dwelling within us impacts our lives is by releasing us from self-centredness and a preoccupation with our problems. Many never get beyond their own difficulties; they seem constantly tied up with them. People have often told me that each time an occasion arises when they could be of help to someone, they are stopped by the inhibitions that spring up from within: their minds and hearts are too much in a whirl to help. Christ has not conquered them and, in turn, they do not have the power to conquer anything. To conquer, we must be conquered; to love, we must first be loved; to serve, we must first be served. All these things Christ offers to do for us.

Lord Jesus, You who never allowed Your own concerns and problems to inhibit You from reaching out to the many who crowded around You, give me that ability too. Amen.

The leisured heart

FOR READING AND MEDITATION
ISAIAH 26:1–15

'You will keep in perfect peace him whose mind is steadfast, because he trusts in you.' (v.3)

Jesus approached life responsibly, passionately, decisively, but also with a calm and confident spirit. He was busy and travelled a good deal, but He always had time for people and their needs. His secret was that He trusted His Father with every detail of His life. 'Do you believe I can take you safely across a high wire in my wheelbarrow?' said Blondin, the tightrope walker, to a little boy who sat watching his act with amazement. 'Oh yes,' said the boy, 'of course I do.' 'Then get into the wheelbarrow,' invited Blondin. 'No fear,' was the reply. The boy believed – but only so far. Trust is believing all the way. And those who trust like that experience the joy of the leisured heart.

Lord Jesus Christ, You moved through life with a leisured heart. May I also have that same confidence of spirit and that same degree of trust in my Father. Amen.

Three Christian types

FOR READING AND MEDITATION
COLOSSIANS 3:1–17

'For you died, and your life is now hidden with Christ in God.' (v.3)

Many Christians live 'on account of', instead of 'in spite of'. One writer says that there are three types of Christians: the rowing boat type, the sailboat type, and the engine-driven type. The rowing boat type is the person who makes a show of being Christian but, when under test, prefers to lean on his or her own powers. The sailboat type depends on the winds. If the winds are with them, they get on, but if not, they stay still. The engine-driven type has power on the inside and they go on whether the winds are favourable or not. They are not self-dependent, circumstance-dependent, but Christ-dependent. And being Christ-dependent they are, in turn, dependable.

Jesus, You kept going when life turned to such roughness that it meant dying upon a cross. Take hold of me so that I might know that same power also; the power to go on – 'in spite of'. Amen.

Power over every sin

FOR READING AND MEDITATION
ROMANS 13:1–14

'... do not think about how to gratify the desires of the
sinful nature.' (v.14)

Another result of our Lord's indwelling us is that we
have power over sin. One of the greatest difficulties
to overcome in pastoral counselling is the moral fatalism
that says in regard to one's sin: 'What could I do? I
am just a human being like everyone else!' The tyranny
of that fatalism must be broken if we are going to be
'more than conquerors'. In the very depths of our being
– note I say 'depths', for a mere surface acceptance is
not enough – we must get hold of the idea that though
we can never reach a point in this life where it is not
possible to sin, we can have a relationship with Jesus
Christ through which it becomes possible not to sin. We
must provide not for failure, but for victory.

*Father, no word of Yours has as much power as that which
opens up for me the possibility of victory over sin. Help me
to be as free from sin as it is possible to be. Amen.*

Fighting! Fighting!

FOR READING AND MEDITATION
MATTHEW 3:1–17

'He will baptise you with the Holy Spirit and with fire.'
(v.11)

M any Christians live strained spiritual lives in the sense that they try too hard to be good. Their fists are clenched, their teeth set, their backs are to the wall – they are fighting, fighting, fighting. It is all very earnest, but not very inviting. In addition, of course, it is very wearing on the person who is acting in this way. All strain means drain. Just as soft metal is strengthened by fire to resist pressure, so we need an inner strength to resist pressure naturally without fighting. You see, life is rarely broken from without; it is broken from within. The presence of this fire-baptising Christ in our hearts is essential if all inner strain is to be taken away.

Jesus, although You were put under pressure, You never broke. Put me through this fiery baptism till all strain is taken out. I consent to Your fire, for I know it means freedom. Amen.

More than conquerors

FOR READING AND MEDITATION
1 CORINTHIANS 15:35–58

'But thanks be to God! He gives us the victory through our Lord Jesus Christ.' (v.57)

Today we end our meditations on the theme 'More than Conquerors' as tomorrow we move into a meditation for the Christmas season. To sum up, if I was asked to put the formula for victorious living into one sentence it would be this: To be a conqueror in Christ means first and foremost to be conquered by Christ. Those who do not allow themselves to be invaded by Christ and His love will find themselves lacking the unified personality that we talked about earlier. In the unified personality the will, emotions, and mind are captured by Christ and the reins of those otherwise wild and untamed 'horses' of evil are put in His powerful hands. Allow His love to conquer you and you can conquer anything!

Father, I see so clearly now that I can never conquer anything outside of me until You have been allowed to conquer everything inside of me. I open my heart again to You. Amen.

'The great divide'

FOR READING AND MEDITATION
JOHN 1:1–14

'The Word became flesh and lived for a while among us.'
(v.14)

N ow we move on to a special Christmas theme: *Why God Became a Baby*. It is here that the uniqueness of Christ and Christianity is so beautifully expressed. The phrase 'The Word became flesh' has been described as 'The Great Divide of Christianity' because it separates the Christian faith from every other religion on the face of the earth. In all other religions the emphasis is on man's search for God; in Christianity the emphasis is on God's search for man. The Infinite has become Incarnate, the Eternal has been contracted to a span. At that first Christmas 2,000 years ago one of the greatest mysteries of the ages took place – God became a baby.

My Father and my God, I am not able to understand all the implications of Your Incarnation, but I know that what prompted it was Your eternal love. Amen.

'Nothing to equal it'

FOR READING AND MEDITATION
1 TIMOTHY 3:1–16

'He appeared in a body … was preached among the nations, was believed on in the world …' (v.16)

A missionary tells how everything of the gospel he presented to the people was met by the bland response: 'What you say is good, but we have something similar in our sacred books.' Then it dawned upon him that one of the greatest differences between the Christian faith and other religions lies in the fact that God became a baby. When he began to talk about the Incarnation he noticed that their interest and curiosity was aroused. Those who became Christians told him later: 'Our religion contains many words, but we have nothing to equal a Word become flesh.' 'Nothing to equal a Word become flesh.' What a comment! This is what makes Christianity unique – *it is a religion different from all others.*

O God, help me come to a clearer understanding than ever this Christmas time of what makes my faith so different. Give me new insight into the wonder of Your Incarnation. Amen.

The ladder

FOR READING AND MEDITATION
GENESIS 28:10–22

'… he saw a stairway resting on the earth, with its top
reaching to heaven …' (v.12)

In all other religions the Word (that is, the main
thought) is expressed through words that set out to
make its message plain. Those words break down into
philosophies, systems, techniques, and so on. The Word,
therefore, becomes words. Only in Jesus Christ did the
Word become flesh – a Person. Christianity doesn't set
out to show humankind how to extend a ladder up to
God to attain salvation, but claims the ladder has been
dropped down to us out of heaven, and that God Himself
has come down that ladder in the Person of His only
begotten Son. Without this fact the Christian faith is a
Word become word – a philosophy, a system. However,
the fact is Jesus is the Word become flesh.

*Father, how can I put into words the joy that is in my heart
this Christmas time as I realise that because I could not
climb up to You, You climbed down to me? Amen.*

Why 'the Word'?

FOR READING AND MEDITATION
1 JOHN 1:1–10

'… which we have looked at and our hands have touched – this we proclaim concerning the Word of life.' (v.1)

Why did John call Jesus 'the Word'? Well, words are the expression of hidden thoughts. If I should sit here at my computer and not put my thoughts into words, hoping you would catch my ideas intuitively and use them as a devotional stimulus for the day, then you would at this moment be looking at a blank page. Only as hidden thoughts are put into words will they express meaning and, hopefully, contribute to your spiritual growth and development. The hidden God, like hidden thought, cannot be comprehended by human minds unless He communicates Himself through a word. Jesus is that Word, and not just mere descriptive words but the living Word that contains the full and final revelation of God.

Father, much of You is hidden. I cannot clearly read Your intentions, so how could I know You unless You showed Yourself to me? This is exactly what You have done in Jesus. Amen.

The authentic Word

FOR READING AND MEDITATION
HEBREWS 1:1–14

'… he has spoken to us by his Son … through whom he made the universe.' (v.2)

Hasn't God revealed Himself in nature? Yes, but not perfectly, not fully. We look up to God through nature and come to the conclusion that God is Law. The discovery of nuclear energy is said to have turned many scientists to thoughts about God. These scientists, when questioned about God, describe Him as awesome, powerful and dependable. But the full truth about God cannot be seen in the splitting of the atom. It tells us simply about His power. The full truth is found only in Jesus. I am revealed as I put my thoughts into words. But God could not fully reveal Himself by mere words so God became flesh in order to more perfectly reveal Himself. In Jesus God unfolds both His power and His character.

God, forgive us when we try to project our own thoughts into the heavens and call them Your revelation. In Jesus we have an authentic Word – the Word that is greater than human words. Amen.

Imperfect media

FOR READING AND MEDITATION
JOHN 6:41–59

'No-one has seen the Father except the one who is from God …' (v.46)

The message of the Old Testament was perfect, but the channel through which the message came was imperfect. Words too have their inadequacies and imperfections. Words get their meaning from the life that surrounds them. To some the word 'home' will convey love, warmth, affection; to others, hostility, or misery and shame. The word acquires its meaning from life's experiences. When we see words such as 'love', 'God', or 'purity' in a book, what do we do? We read into them our highest experience of those words. But our highest experience of love, for example, is not the highest love; it is partial and incomplete. We only see love at its highest when we see it wrapped up in the life and ministry of Jesus.

Father, I see only faintly whatever lattice I look through, except the lattice and life of Your Son. What I see in Him sets my heart on fire, and I long to behold more and more. Amen.

God's self-revelation

FOR READING AND MEDITATION
JOHN 14:1–14

'Anyone who has seen me has seen the Father.' (v.9)

What do we need for a perfect revelation of God? A life must come among us – a divine life that will put fresh content into the words associated with God. Now when we reflect on the word 'God' we need not rely on our imagination. The nature of God has been uncovered in understandable terms – human terms. For example, we see love and forgiveness not in terms of an imperfect human definition but in the light of a perfect love that prayed for enemies upon a cross: I look up to God through Jesus and I now *know* what God is like because Christ was a true likeness of His Father: He is a good God, a trustworthy God, a loving God. In Jesus we see God as He really is – really is!

O Son of God, thank You for showing us the Father. We would never have known what He was like had we not looked on Your face. Amen.

Jesus – 'God approachable'

FOR READING AND MEDITATION
HEBREWS 2:1–18

'Since the children have flesh and blood, he too shared in their humanity ...' (v.14)

What we find in our upward search for God is not God, but our ideas about Him. We create God in the image of our imagination. No philosopher ever imagined a God who would take a body and become like us in order to redeem us. A love like that just does not exist – at least in the categories of philosophy. In the real world, however, seeing is believing – the Word who was God, and was equal with God, became flesh and dwelt among us. The Son of God became the Son of Man in order that the sons of men might become the sons of God. I love the phrase that I think was first coined by E. Stanley Jones, who described Jesus as 'God approachable'.

My Father and my God, what a marvellous message Christmas contains. It is not about us knocking at the door of heaven, but You knocking at the door of our hearts. Amen.

Jesus' kind of love

FOR READING AND MEDITATION
JOHN 13:12–38

*'A new command I give you: Love one another. As I have
loved you …' (v.34)*

We should beware a movement away from the
Person of Christ to the principles of Christ.
Apart from the Person of Christ the principles would
mean something else. Take today's text for example: 'A
new command I give you: Love one another. As I have
loved you …' Without the last portion – 'As I have
loved you' – there would have been nothing new in the
commandment. The principle of love that had been spelt
out in the Old Testament takes on a new meaning when
set against the backdrop of Christ's Person. Jesus put a
higher meaning into love by the way He loved. When we
take the principles of the Christian faith and ignore the
Person, then we take the stream but not the source, the
rays but not the sun.

*Father, how sad it is that so many want the impersonal
principles rather than the Personal Christ. May others come
to know You as I know You personally. Amen.*

The Divine Shepherd

FOR READING AND MEDITATION
JOHN 10:1–21

'They ... will listen to my voice, and there shall be one flock and one shepherd.' (v.16)

Advocates of the New Age talk about God as 'a Divine Principle'. They may talk to themselves about God, but they cannot talk to God. You cannot talk to a principle; only to a person. A religion founded on the 'Divine Principle' is a religion where you end up talking to yourself. A little child crying in the middle of the night does not want the principle of motherhood but the person of its mother. We cannot say our prayers to a principle or worship an axiom. Prayer and worship are the response on the part of the person to the response of the Person. There can be no communion with a principle, only with a Person. God speaks to us and cares for us as a shepherd cares for his sheep.

Lord, You know my voice and I know Yours. This gives me a joy I just cannot put into words. Thank You, dear Father. Amen.

Christianity is Christ

FOR READING AND MEDITATION
ACTS 4:1–22

'… there is no other name under heaven … by which we must be saved.' (v.12)

The Person of Christ is the Christian faith. Christianity has its doctrines, but it is more than a doctrine; it has its creeds, but it is more than a creed; it has its rites and ceremonies, but it is more than rites or ceremonies; it has its institutions, but it is more than an institution. *Christianity is Christ.* Christian people are people who believe in God, and believe also that the way to God – the only way to God – is through Christ. When we come in contact with the Person – Christ – then the principles embodied in the Person take on power and vitality. We want to practise the principles because He practised and embodied them. Principles become power only as they are embodied in a person.

Gracious Father, You have shown us in Your Son that You practise what You require of us. Let all Your principles become personal in me this day. Amen.

The face

FOR READING AND MEDITATION
I PETER 1:1–12

'Though you have not seen him, you love him …' (v.8)

'Christianity,' said a little boy, 'puts a face on God.' How meaningful those words become at this Christmas season, for Jesus is God's face. What if there were no flesh in the Godhead – no face like my face there? Then the Godhead would be awesome but not attractive. The fact that there is a human face on the throne of God touches my heart in a way that nothing else could. It means I can stand in the presence of God knowing that alongside me will stand One who is like me in every way – Jesus. One who has worn my flesh, measured its frailty, and is swift to save.

O Father, the thought of a human face on the throne of God evokes a response in me that perhaps nothing else could. Jesus is so unlike me yet so like me. Amen.

No fleeting vision

FOR READING AND MEDITATION
LUKE 1:67–80

'Praise be to the Lord … because he has come and has
redeemed his people.' (v.68)

The revelation of God in Christ was not a momentary
rift in the clouds, a fleeting vision of what God is like.
He didn't sit on a cloud and pass on commands, or pick
us up with a kind of celestial tongs and take us to heaven
to avoid soiling His fingers with the messy business of
human living. No. He 'lived for a while among us' – amid
our poverty, amid our temptations, amid our problems
and choices, amid our hopes and disappointments. He
lived among us and showed us how to live – by living,
not simply lecturing. He revealed the character of God in
operation in the same surroundings where your character
and mine are wrought out here on earth. He lived with
total dependence on the Father for thirty-three years.

Lord Jesus, how glad I am that I walk with One who has
all the wisdom, all the power, all the grace I need. Now
I know what life can be like for I have seen it – in You.
Amen.

A day for thanksgiving

FOR READING AND MEDITATION
MATTHEW 1:18–25

'… you are to give him the name Jesus, because he will save his people from their sins.' (v.21)

On this, the day we set apart to celebrate in a special way the birth of Christ, how good it is to know we are celebrating not the birth of a principle, but the birth of a Person. This is the meaning of Christmas. Jesus is Immanuel – God with us. We did not dare dream that God was like Christ. But He is. Just as one can analyse a tiny sunbeam and discover within it the chemical make-up of the sun, so we look at the character of Jesus and know what God's character is like. The Christmas word must become flesh in me. I must be a miniature Christmas. The Christian spirit is the Christmas spirit extended throughout the whole year.

Gracious Father, let someone see in me the meaning of being a Christian. May I be the Christmas message. And not just today but every day. In Christ's name I pray. Amen.

Among us

FOR READING AND MEDITATION
HEBREWS 4:1–16

'... *tempted in every way, just as we are – yet ... without sin.*' *(v.15)*

Our Lord really dwelt *among* us. The first temptation in the wilderness was to live *apart* from us, by using power that was not available to ordinary mortals. This Jesus rejected – He would eat as we eat. The second temptation – to live *above* us – this He rejected also. He would not throw Himself down from the pinnacle of the Temple and then be carried back by angels. That would be living *above* the rest of humanity. The third temptation was to live *as* we live, by taking the devil's suggestion to worship him, to adopt his methods, and thus gain the kingdoms of the world. He rejected this temptation because although He identified with us in every way, He would not commit sin.

Lord Jesus, I know that You know me, not just from the outside, but from the inside also. You dwelt 'among' us. Not 'apart', not 'above', not 'as'. Amen.

See His glory

FOR READING AND MEDITATION
JOHN 17:1–19

*'I have brought you glory on earth by completing the work
you gave me to do.' (v.4)*

When John wrote, 'We have seen his glory' (John
1:14), what did he mean? What would that 'glory'
be? Our Lord's glory was not so much in what He did or
what He said but in who He was. Look at the words
once again: 'the glory of the one and only, who came
from the Father'. His glory flowed from His uniqueness
as 'the one and only'. It was intrinsic, something that
flowed out of Him and permeated everything He did.
He certainly demonstrated glory in His knowledge, and
glory in His wisdom, and glory in His deeds, but the real
glory lay in who He was – the glory of being. Knowledge,
might, wisdom, power and all the other qualities flowed
from His being. Being the 'Son' was everything.

*Lord Jesus, I praise You not only for what You did and what
You said but for who You are. You are the only Son: the only
Incarnation of the glorious God. Amen.*

A sinner's favourite word

FOR READING AND MEDITATION
TITUS 2:1–15

'For the grace of God that brings salvation has appeared to all men.' (v.11)

The first characteristic of God is love, and grace is love at work. The first element in the Christian faith is 'grace' – an act of outgoing, forgiving love. Grace is love favouring us when we are not favourable, loving us when we are not lovable, accepting us when we are not acceptable, redeeming us when, in human terms, and by all the rules of the book, we are not redeemable. John Wallace used to say that although the favourite word of angels might be love, the favourite word of sinners is grace. Love reaches out on the same level, he explained, but grace is a word with a stoop in it. Grace always bends to pick one up. Grace is love applied, the Word of love become flesh.

Father, I praise You above all for Your grace. Thank You for favouring me when I was not favourable, and loving me when I was unlovable. In Jesus' name. Amen.

Love is first

FOR READING AND MEDITATION
PHILIPPIANS 2:1–11

'And being found in appearance as a man, he humbled himself and became obedient to death …' (v.8)

There is nothing wrong in saying that 'God is truth', but that is not the first quality to recognise in the Deity. The first characteristic of God is love. If Scripture had said, 'God is truth', then people would regard Christianity as a philosophy. But the Christian faith is not first and foremost a thought, a philosophy, but an act – an act of love invading history to redeem lost men and women. It is grace in action. Truth does come into the picture, of course, but it comes after grace. I think this is because in order to understand truth we have to 'see' it, not just hear about it. Grace is truth in gracious action. We see the nature of truth through the act – the Word made flesh.

Lord Jesus, You not only said, 'I am the truth', but showed us through Your acts what truth is all about – not a dry proposition but something liveable and lovable. Amen.

Truth is second

FOR READING AND MEDITATION
1 CORINTHIANS 10:23–33

'... *whatever you do, do it all for the glory of God.*' (v.31)

When it comes to describing God as both truth and grace (John 1:14) then we need to put grace first. But although 'grace' is first, 'truth' has to be second. Grace must not be seen as maudlin sentimentality for it works within the framework of integrity and truth. Headhunters in Borneo who had become Christians said: 'Christianity is the only faith where you can't wangle God to get benefits out of Him.' They were used to a faith where you could cajole, bribe, manipulate and wangle your god to get him to do you favours. Not so with Christ. We surrender to Him, follow Him, obey Him, and our blessing takes care of itself. It is a consequence, not a cause, of our surrender.

Lord Jesus, You are both grace and truth. This means I cannot bribe You, wangle You, or manipulate You. But I can come to You honestly, obeying Your laws, and get everything I need. Amen.

Flawless character

FOR READING AND MEDITATION
2 CORINTHIANS 5:11-21

'God made him who had no sin to be sin for us …' (v.21)

When John told us that Jesus is *full* of grace and truth he was saying that in Him there was no room for their opposites. He is one character, and only one. Over the years I have met some wonderful Christians, but the more I have got to know and relate to them, the clearer their imperfections have become. No doubt the same could be said by others about me. What is my point? This – Christians have spotty characters; some are more 'spotty' than others. Jesus, however, was not nearly perfect; He was absolutely perfect. No one could find a flaw in Him. He is not only the best humanity has ever seen, but the best it will ever see. He is *full* of grace and truth.

O Father, let the beauty of Jesus' character be seen also in me. Now and evermore. For the honour and glory of Your name I ask it. Amen.

National Distributors

UK: (and countries not listed below)
CWR, Waverley Abbey House, Waverley Lane, Farnham, Surrey GU9 8EP.
Tel: (01252) 784700 Outside UK (44) 1252 784700

AUSTRALIA: CMC Australasia, PO Box 519, Belmont, Victoria 3216.
Tel: (03) 5241 3288 Fax: (03) 5241 3290

CANADA: David C Cook Distribution Canada, PO Box 98, 55 Woodslee Avenue, Paris, Ontario N3L 3E5.
Tel: 1800 263 2664

GHANA: Challenge Enterprises of Ghana, PO Box 5723, Accra.
Tel: (021) 222437/223249 Fax: (021) 226227

HONG KONG: Cross Communications Ltd, 1/F, 562A Nathan Road, Kowloon.
Tel: 2780 1188 Fax: 2770 6229

INDIA: Crystal Communications, 10-3-18/4/1, East Marredpalli, Secunderabad - 500026, Andhra Pradesh.
Tel/Fax: (040) 27737145

KENYA: Keswick Books and Gifts Ltd, PO Box 10242, Nairobi.
Tel: (02) 331692/226047 Fax: (02) 728557

MALAYSIA: Salvation Book Centre (M) Sdn Bhd, 23 Jalan SS 2/64, 47300 Petaling Jaya, Selangor.
Tel: (03) 78766411/78766797 Fax: (03) 78757066/78756360

NEW ZEALAND: CMC Australasia, PO Box 303298, North Harbour, Auckland 0751.
Tel: 0800 449 408 Fax: 0800 449 049

NIGERIA: FBFM, Helen Baugh House, 96 St Finbarr's College Road, Akoka, Lagos.
Tel: (01) 7747429/4700218/825775/827264

PHILIPPINES: OMF Literature Inc, 776 Boni Avenue, Mandaluyong City.
Tel: (02) 531 2183 Fax: (02) 531 1960

SINGAPORE: Alby Commercial Enterprises Pte Ltd, 95 Kallang Avenue #04-00, AIS Industrial Building, 339420.
Tel: (65) 629 27238 Fax: (65) 629 27235

SOUTH AFRICA: Struik Christian Books, 80 MacKenzie Street, PO Box 1144, Cape Town 8000.
Tel: (021) 462 4360 Fax: (021) 461 3612

SRI LANKA: Christombu Publications (Pvt) Ltd, Bartleet House, 65 Braybrooke Place, Colombo 2.
Tel: (9411) 2421073/2447665

TANZANIA: CLC Christian Book Centre, PO Box 1384, Mkwepu Street, Dar es Salaam.
Tel/Fax: (022) 2119439

USA: David C Cook Distribution Canada, PO Box 98, 55 Woodslee Avenue, Paris, Ontario N3L 3E5, Canada.
Tel: 1800 263 2664

ZIMBABWE: Word of Life Books (Pvt) Ltd, Christian Media Centre, 8 Aberdeen Road, Avondale,
PO Box A480 Avondale, Harare. Tel: (04) 333355 or 091301188

For email addresses, visit the CWR website: www.cwr.org.uk

CWR is a Registered Charity – Number 294387

CWR is a Limited Company registered in England – Registration Number 1990308

Day and Residential Courses
Counselling Training
Leadership Development
Biblical Study Courses
Regional Seminars
Ministry to Women
Daily Devotionals
Books and Videos
Conference Centre

Trusted all Over the World

CWR HAS GAINED A WORLDWIDE reputation as a centre of excellence for Bible-based training and resources. From our headquarters at Waverley Abbey House, Farnham, England, we have been serving God's people for over 40 years with a vision to help apply God's Word to everyday life and relationships. The daily devotional *Every Day with Jesus* is read by nearly a million readers an issue in more than 150 countries, and our unique courses in biblical studies and pastoral care are respected all over the world. Waverley Abbey House provides a conference centre in a tranquil setting.

For free brochures on our seminars and courses, conference facilities, or a catalogue of CWR resources, please contact us at the following address. CWR, Waverley Abbey House, Waverley Lane, Farnham, Surrey GU9 8EP, UK

Telephone: +44 (0)1252 784700
Email: mail@cwr.org.uk
Website: www.cwr.org.uk

CWR Applying God's Word to everyday life and relationships

Other great Pocket Devotionals

Perfect for travel or to give as gifts

Only £7.99 each

Living Hope
ISBN: 978-1-85345-464-6

Walking in Faith
ISBN: 978-1-85345-399-1

Joy for Today
ISBN: 978-1-85345-398-4

For more details visit:
www.cwr.org.uk/pd

Every Day with Jesus

This is one of the most popular daily Bible study tools in the world, with around one million readers each issue. This inspiring devotional is available bimonthly in regular or large-print format and as a six-part annual subscription.

- Get practical help with life's challenges
- Gain insight into the deeper truths of Scripture
- Be challenged, comforted and encouraged
- Study six topics in depth each year

STANDARD
Format: 120 x 170mm, 72-page booklet
Published date: bimonthly
ISSN: 0967-1889
£2.25 each
£12.50 UK annual subscription
(6 issues)

LARGE PRINT
Format: A4, 72-page booklet
ISSN: 0967-4381
£2.25 each
£12.50 UK annual subscription
(6 issues)

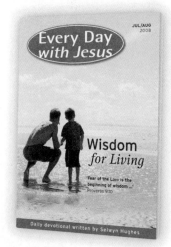

Prices correct at time of printing